Servants of the Spirit:
Portraits of Pentecostal/Charismatic Pioneers
Edited by Andrea Johnson

Copyright © 2010 by OBC Publishing
Published in Des Moines, Iowa, by OBC Publishing

Library of Congress Catalog Card Number: 2010902185
ISBN 978-0-9608160-7-1; 0-9608160-7-0

Book and cover design by Greg Roberts

Printed in the United States of America
First Edition 2010

Servants
OF THE
Spirit

*Portraits of Pentecostal/
Charismatic Pioneers*

Foreword by

JACK HAYFORD

Edited by Andrea Johnson

 Published by OBC Publishing

Dedicated to

BISHOP JERRY MACKLIN

The Executive Committee of the Pentecostal/
Charismatic Churches of North America gratefully
dedicates *Servants of the Spirit: Portraits of Pentecostal/
Charismatic Pioneers* to Bishop Jerry Macklin,
founder and senior pastor of
Glad Tidings Church of God in Christ,
Hayward, California.

Bishop Macklin served as Chairman of PCCNA
from October 2006 to October 2009.
During his tenure he cast the vision and
provided inspiration for this book.
At the time of this printing Bishop Macklin serves
as Co-Chairman of the PCCNA and is on the
General Board of the Church of God in Christ serving
as Second Assistant Presiding Bishop.

CONTENTS

A CONTINUING MOVEMENT AND ITS BEGINNINGS

Dr. Jack W. Hayford

You are stepping into a cluster of miracle stories – of remarkable experiences of individuals who "met God" and discovered He would do far more with them and those they influenced than they ever could have imagined or caused to happen.

You will find here the same thing so often seen in the Bible and throughout Church history: God delights to take ordinary people who yield to His will and believe His Word, and through them work extraordinary things – works unto His glory and to the magnifying of His Son, Jesus Christ the Lord!

These are among tens of thousands of stories that stretch across the ages. Each is an account of how faithfulness, sacrifice, a love for the gospel of Christ and a will to spread it have been fused into individuals whose impact has birthed movements that stand today as a continuing demonstration of the power of God at work among His people. The distinctive and the common bond of these stories is that they reflect the founding stories and continuing testimony of several organizations that fellowship in unity as a part of the Pentecostal and Charismatic Churches of North America (PCCNA).

The influence of these "movements within a Movement" has its birth in the revival that rose with an amazing outbreak and spread – beginning over a hundred years ago. Since its beginnings, the "Pentecostal-Charismatic Movement" has not only reflected a holy tidal wave of a divinely granted "amazing grace" of blessing, but also has become a focal point of studies for more than its influence and impact on the Church and the religious world in general.

Sociologists and historians research and tabulate the cultural transformations and societal benefits that the Holy Spirit of God has worked where "the whole gospel for the whole man" has been preached, ministered, and applied with fidelity to God's Word and a dependency upon His Spirit's power.

Present day studies are unfolding more than a panorama of past growth, but note the dramatic role of Pentecostal-charismatics as a force that has basically "moved the epicenter of Christianity to the southern hemisphere of the planet." The glory of that global spread through evangelism, sent from the western world to the developing nations through the years, is not the victory of a religion or of politics. It has come about because it brings individual human transformation and victory, lifting souls above the despair of futility unto a recovery of meaning, identity, and functionality. This includes people who have been brought into a practical (and sometimes miraculous) discovery of health and wholeness in all of life – all features of their transformation and reorientation to life being by reason of their coming to the knowledge of God's love, life, and grace through His Son, Jesus Christ.

It is *both* the story behind and the impact of individuals and groups that have contributed to this socio-cultural phenomenon that makes this book pragmatic. But it is in retracing the way God moved upon the hearts and through the lives of people He was raising up to change the world that makes it *dynamic*.

And thus, it is into these pages I invite you – to read and to discover or to be reminded again, that:

> "*The eyes of the Lord run to and fro throughout the whole earth, to show Himself strong on behalf of those whose heart is loyal to Him*" (2 Chronicles 16:9, NKJ).

That loyalty springs from an abandonment to God's will and a surrender to His Spirit, to the way of His Word and to a humility of dependency upon Him.

From these individuals have risen organizations that continue –

generations after their founder has passed on. That continuity in purpose, power, and purity is only explainable by one feature: their will to continue in the same surrender, obedience, and humility, the will to "receive power from on high," to "be witnesses…unto the ends of the earth" in the name of Jesus.

In the confidence that God will attend the testimony of the works and workers (because the goal of honoring them is so that larger honor be given to the works of God's hand and the wonders of His Spirit glorifying Christ throughout the earth) this volume is placed before you here.

May its message multiply in and through you – unto great joy, increasing blessing and the extending of God's Kingdom of love throughout the earth.

An Amazing Grace – Unending!

The twentieth century realized a series of "waves of revival" that transcended regional or national impact – evidencing at least four discernible "times of refreshing from the Lord." It is neither sectarian nor self-serving to the purposes of this book to simply observe that the common denominator of them all has been the grace of God that was manifest through leaders, networks, denominations, and groups who were dominantly "Pentecostal." The term mandates definition to verify the assertion as you open these pages, because the reports constituting the history being referenced do not always indicate themselves by that term or designation.

The rise of the "Pentecostal" movement, like so many other revival eras in Church history, did not come about as a quest to form either a separate or separatistic grouping of believers or churches. Those engaged in and receiving a fresh visitation from God – especially at points at which He not only is renewing but also is seeking to reawaken His people to His Word and His Spirit – seem to inevitably find less than a full receptivity among His own. Thus, what began – and manifestly was – a revival that was affecting believers in all parts of the Church became a distinct movement, and there was other than a sectarian reason those within it called themselves "Pentecostals."

It was simple: What was happening among them was birthed in the same way the Church was born on the day of Pentecost – a term derived from Acts, chapter 2 – the fiftieth day after the Jewish Passover. To this day, Jewish tradition still observes the Feast of Shavuot (i.e.), "weeks"; being the day following "a week of weeks" (7x7 days), arriving at the day observed as "first-fruits" – the beginning of harvest. Shavuot also celebrates the giving of the Law at Mount Sinai, fifty days after God delivered Israel from Egypt and the first Passover occurred.

While the Acts 2 outpouring of the Holy Spirit upon the Church was attended by all those present beginning "to speak with tongues as the Spirit gave them utterance," this profound experience (also often called "glossolalia") was neither the only nor the foremost reason "Pentecostals" adopted their name in the early 1900s. While critics refusing to accept the contemporary works of the Holy Spirit evidencing His reviving presence in this way, "speaking with tongues" has been but an introductory point in the perspective of Pentecostal people from that day to this. To be "Pentecostal" is also:

- *To be filled (or baptized with) the Holy Spirit.*
- *To make disciples and teach them "all that Jesus commanded."*
- *To focus and engage the global harvest with evangelistic passion.*
- *To embrace "all the counsel of God" in the Scriptures.*
- *To meet human need with generosity and compassion in giving and sharing.*
- *To meet human sickness and bondage with Christ's healing and deliverance.*
- *To answer the Spirit's call to holiness of life and a readiness for Christ's return.*

These only begin to summarize the *life and breath* of God's Holy Spirit as He moved in the first century Church as seen in the

Book of Acts and the Epistles, but the lifestyle that was begotten among those believers *began with Pentecost*. They were a people who were an extension of the traits, priorities, and spiritual quest of those at the beginning, and it is that fact that occasioned the name of a movement as "the Pentecostals."

From the twentieth century revival which received that designation, at least three general seasons of similar awakening – *re-awakening*, if you will – are generally acknowledged: (1) the Azusa Street revival, (2) the Latter Rain revival, and (3) the Charismatic renewal. Generally speaking, the first was from early 1900s and into the "teens" of the century. The second began shortly after WWII and extended into the 1960s. The third was sparked in the sixties, but essentially spread during the 1970s and the 1980s. With the passage of these years, a variation in terminology began, with a refinement and clarity of theology occasioning some of the changes while at the same time finding increasing impact and welcome throughout the larger Body of Christ. Today, millions of "Spirit-filled" or "charismatic" believers are members in congregations of every tradition, while at the same time a rapid expansion in growth through evangelism and church multiplication is found among and through those denominations founded during the earlier era of this global movement.

Beginning in the "19-teens" the first, formally organized and convened "Pentecostal denominations" came into existence. Just as many "networks of churches" today would spurn the term "denomination," so it was with the early Pentecostals. However, frankness with the term itself inevitably occasions most revivalist groups to honestly acknowledge, "we are a group with a name and our own distinctive 'family style,' and it is simply the presence of that family identity that is inherent in the "nom" (name) or "de-nom-ing" (naming) of a group. Thus, and contrary to the sometimes slurring of the idea of "denomination" as though it automatically indicated an absence, if not a resistance, to revival, this book is largely a summary of the beginnings and current continuation of the reviving work of the Holy Spirit in several groups of Pentecostal churches who still perpetuate in their midst the revival spirit from which they were born – many reaching back to the beginnings of the "Pentecostal movement."

These stories aren't the end, but they give evidence that it continues with an ever expanding result. The sum of it to date is but a prophecy that is still being fulfilled. It is related in John's Gospel, chapter 7:37-39 (NKJ), where he records the words of Jesus spoken at one of the last feasts He attended in Jerusalem only months before His death, resurrection, and ascension:

> "On the last day, that great day of the feast, Jesus stood and cried out saying, *'If anyone thirsts, let him come to Me and drink. He that believes in Me, as the Scripture has said, out of his heart (inmost being) will flow rivers of living water.'* But this He spoke concerning the Spirit, whom those believing in Him would receive; for Jesus was not yet glorified."

And so it has been to this day: The outpouring of the Spirit at Pentecost released a stream that continues relentlessly – spreading wider and deeper, just as the prophet Ezekiel described it would be (47:1-9). The testimonies of unending grace here are but a few among the multitudes that continue, as the stream flows from that Upper Room into each of our hearts today.

Read … receive … and welcome the River's continuing – through you!

Dr. Jack W. Hayford
Founding Pastor, The Church On The Way
Chancellor, The King's College and Seminary
Past President, International Foursquare Churches

ACKNOWLEDGMENTS AND APOLOGIES

The pioneers of Pentecostal/Charismatic movements were dynamic, colorful men and women of faith. Like the disciples in the *Book of Acts*, a fire consumed their being with an unquenchable thirst for the power of the Holy Spirit and a passion to reach the nations. Though not without fault, their influence is undisputed and probably not fully appreciated. Yet their legacy lingers in the movements they initiated. *Servants of the Spirit* allows these movements, each in their own way, to tell the stories of their own cherished and beloved founders.

The goal of this volume is not a compilation of facts and dates, though most are accurate and extant. Rather, it is a storytelling of these remarkable founders. As each of the writers of the Gospels viewed first century events from a different perspective, the authors of this book share their stories from personal vantage points as well. And though each movement strives for accuracy in the recording of their history, some have found their early leaders, fervent in their quest to spread the Good News, took little time to record their actions, making it difficult to corroborate dates. Photos were provided by organizations. Due to the archival nature of these photographs, quality varies. Additionally, most individuals' titles were not provided to the editor; therefore, for the sake of consistency and accuracy we chose not to use titles except when mentioned in the text.

We are grateful to each of the writers, denominational leaders, and staff who worked diligently to gather biographies, photos, and facts. We are especially indebted to the writers, who brought those facts to life. A huge thank you goes to Jack Hayford for authoring a comprehensive, compelling foreword.

Appreciation must also be expressed to Wayne Warner, for providing his expertise in historical editing. Additional proofreading and manuscript preparation assistance was provided by Delores Winegar, Leslee Simmons, Andrew Farmer, and Julie Patten. Special acknowledgement goes to Greg Roberts for his capable handling of the graphic design and layout. I am thankful for Denny, my husband, who graciously assumed extra household duties to enable me to work on this project. Jeff Farmer, President of Open Bible Churches and architect of this project, deserves our utmost gratitude, as well as Mary Johnston, his assistant.

Our highest praise and glory go to God the Father, Jesus Christ His Son, and to the Holy Spirit, who empowers us for service.

Andrea Johnson, 2010

CHAPTER 1

Assemblies *of* God

AG

FOUNDERS:

Eudorus N. Bell (right) with
J. Roswell Flower

**J. Roswell and Alice
Reynolds Flower**

LAYING THE FOUNDATION FOR THE ASSEMBLIES OF GOD:
Eudorus Bell and Alice and J. Roswell Flower

By Darrin Rodgers and David Ringer

The tumultuous world of early Pentecostalism was marked not only by passionate proclamation of the gospel, but in many quarters by a certain impermanence, impetuosity, and lack of wisdom. Responding to these problems, the General Council of the Assemblies of God (USA) was organized in 1914 by a broad coalition of ministers who recognized the need to provide accountability on doctrine, morals, and finances, and also to establish institutions such as schools, a publishing house, and a missionary agency.[1] With echoes from the iconic Pentecostal revivals at Topeka and Azusa Street still ringing in their ears, the founding fathers and mothers of the Assemblies of God came together in Hot Springs, Arkansas, April 2-12, 1914, and laid the foundation for what would become one of the largest families of Pentecostal churches in the world.[2]

Participants at the first General Council represented a variety of independent churches and loosely organized networks of ministers from across the country, enabling them to form the first truly national Pentecostal body in the United States. Delegates elected leaders within two of these networks to serve as the young organization's first officers. Eudorus N. Bell, a leader in the Church of God in Christ,[3] was elected to serve as general chairman. J. Roswell Flower, a leader in the Association of Christian Assemblies in Indiana, became the first secretary. Both men had broad spheres of influence, partly because each published prominent Pentecostal newspapers, which became the official organs of the Assemblies of God.

The governance of the Assemblies of God has always been driven by its grassroots constituency. The fellowship has never had a larger-than-life leader whose personality was interchangeable with the organization's identity – not a Luther or a Calvin, or an A. J. Tomlinson (Church of God, Cleveland, Tennessee) or a Charles H. Mason (Church of God in Christ). Still, the influence of E. N. Bell and J. Roswell and Alice (Reynolds) Flower set the trajectory for the development of the Assemblies of God.

Eudorus N. Bell

Eudorus N. Bell (1866-1923) was elected to serve as the first general chairman of the General Council of the Assemblies of God at its founding convention in Hot Springs, Arkansas, in April 1914.[4] In some ways, Bell was the natural choice. He, along with five other Church of God in Christ leaders from various south central states, had first issued the open invitation to Pentecostals to organize a general council in December 1913 in his newspaper, *Word and Witness*.[5] By March 1914, 34 Pentecostal leaders from across the United States and Egypt and from various organizations had signed onto this call. [6]

Eudorus N. Bell emerged from humble circumstances. Bell and his twin brother, Endorus, were born in Lake Butler, Florida. Their father died two years later. The Bell family experienced dire poverty and Eudorus worked hard to help make ends meet. J. Roswell Flower later remarked that "these early days of struggle developed in him that sterling, rugged character" for which Eudorus later became known as a Pentecostal leader.[7]

At an early age, Eudorus accepted Christ and felt called to the ministry. He enrolled at Stetson University in the 1890s, embarking upon an educational journey that would later earn him the distinction of being one of the better educated clergy among the first generation of American Pentecostals. In 1900, Bell matriculated at Southern Baptist Theological Seminary in Louisville, Kentucky. Two years later he transferred to the University of Chicago Divinity School (then a Baptist school), where he completed his B.A. in 1903. Upon his graduation, he accepted the pastorate of a Baptist church in Fort Worth, Texas.

In 1907, Eudorus heard about the emerging Pentecostal revival. Taking a leave of absence from his Fort Worth church, he returned to Chicago to spend time at the North Avenue Mission, pastored by Baptist-turned-Pentecostal William Durham. Durham's church had become an important revival center in American Pentecostalism following his trip to the Azusa Street revival where he was baptized in the Spirit. Eudorus found the Pentecostal message and experience compelling, but he needed time to sort out the theological issues. After seeking God for 11 months in Chicago, he received his personal Pentecost and spoke in tongues on July 18, 1908.[8]

Eudorus returned to Fort Worth and offered his resignation. The church asked him to stay, which he did for another year. In 1909, at age 43, Eudorus married a widow, Katie Kimbrough, who had three children. That same year the family moved to Malvern, Arkansas, where Eudorus served his first Pentecostal pastorate. He identified with the Apostolic Faith Movement (renamed Church of God in Christ), a Pentecostal organization that had grown to a couple hundred ministers after breaking away from Charles Parham in 1907. Bell became the publisher of that group's newspaper, called *The Apostolic Faith* (renamed *Word and Witness*).

Bell's Influence on the Assemblies of God

Eudorus contributed significantly to the development of the Assemblies of God, despite living for only nine years after its formation. In addition to serving as chairman (1914 and 1920-1923), Eudorus edited the two official periodicals of the Assemblies of God and wrote extensively about polity and doctrine.

Eudorus Bell identified what he believed to be three key organizational principles for the Assemblies of God in a tract-sized pamphlet, *General Council Principles*.[9] First, he argued that the formation of the General Council was scriptural, following the pattern of the early Church. Second, he held that the General Council should be non-sectarian. It should avoid attempts to legislate details in doctrine and practice, leaving districts and congregations free to determine these. "[F]undamental teachings and New Testament order" are matters for General Council determination; but, beyond these district councils, local congregations, and ministers are free to "adapt to local situations," he instructed.[10] The third Council principle was the commitment to a voluntary fellowship. Eudorus remarked about the Hot Springs meeting, "There was nothing compelling anybody to come…; nothing compelling them to take part after they got there, and nothing compels them to keep on taking part."[11]

Eudorus also made an impact on the Assemblies of God understandings of Christology, sanctification, and the baptism in the Holy Spirit. There is a certain irony to his contributions concerning Christology, as he initially threw his support to the emerging Oneness movement before it rejected the doctrine of the Trinity. Eudorus was rebaptized in 1915 using the formula "in the name of Jesus," instead of the traditional Trinitarian formulation. But he distanced himself from this movement once it moved beyond a simple preference for a baptismal formula. His rebaptism highlighted doctrinal divisions within the young Assemblies of God and the broader Pentecostal movement. In response, the 1916 General Council adopted the Statement of Fundamental Truths, which set forth its basic theological beliefs, including an affirmation of Trinitarian orthodoxy.[12]

Eudorus also helped to shape the Assemblies of God view that sanctification is progressive. Eudorus sided with Durham, who was probably best known for disputing the Wesleyan-Holiness concept of "entire sanctification," which claimed that perfection was attainable in the Christian life. In a piece identified as the "last message he wrote," Eudorus argued that "some hurtful theories and practices" arose from the belief that the old nature could be fully eradicated.[13]

Bell's own experience of Spirit baptism was in line with Parham's model of tongues as the "Bible evidence" of the baptism in the Holy Spirit. Eudorus defended this view and asserted, "The

General Council holds solidly for speaking in tongues as the Spirit of God gives utterance as the external physical sign of the completed baptism in the Holy Ghost. This is our distinctive testimony."[14] When later asked if a person might "receive the baptism one night, and then not speak in tongues until four months afterward," he acknowledged that some people report such experiences; however, he answered that the New Testament provides no such example. If such experiences do occur, they are "abnormal." Eudorus suggested two possible explanations: (1) the person "wrongfully NAMED this experience;" or (2) the experience was not "a completed baptism."[15]

J. Roswell Flower and Alice Reynolds Flower

J. Roswell Flower (1888-1970) was born in Canada. His parents were warmhearted Methodists who, at the turn of the century, moved to Zion City, Illinois, the Utopian community founded by faith healer John Alexander Dowie. However, the Flowers soon became disenchanted with Dowie's teaching and behavior and moved to Indianapolis, Indiana. J. Roswell showed little interest in spiritual matters during the family's stay in Illinois. When the Pentecostal fire from Azusa Street came to Indianapolis in 1907, though, the tinder of his heart was ignited.

Alice Marie Reynolds (1890-1991) was born into a family that experienced divine healing firsthand. Alice's mother had been miraculously healed on her deathbed several years prior to Alice's birth. At age 17, on Easter Sunday of 1908, Alice was among the first to be baptized in the Holy Spirit in Indianapolis. J. Roswell, who was also at the Indianapolis meetings, heard young people singing in the Spirit. This touched his heart, and he yielded to Christ. Alice Reynolds also touched his heart.

J. Roswell and Alice married on June 1, 1911, and immediately launched into evangelistic ministry. Both wielded significant influence in the young Pentecostal movement through their prolific pens and publications. When J. Roswell Flower attended the founding General Council in Hot Springs, Arkansas, in April 1914, he was elected to serve as secretary at the young age of 25. By his retirement in December 1959, J. Roswell Flower had become one of the most recognizable names in the Assemblies of God, having served in every Assemblies of God executive office, except that of general superintendent.

Unlike Bell, J. Roswell Flower's formal education had ended in early high school. Alice, however, was a high school graduate and studied at least one semester at Butler University in Indianapolis. As a married couple, J. Roswell and Alice studied at D. Wesley Myland's short-term Gibeah Bible School in Plainfield, Indiana; both were ordained into the ministry by Myland at the end of their training in 1913.[16]

The Flowers' Influence on the Assemblies of God

J. Roswell and Alice Reynolds Flower left an indelible impression upon the Assemblies of God. First, their home life bore witness to the sanctifying power of the Holy Spirit. Out of that life flowed Alice's sermons, articles, and books on the Christian home. Of their six children, five entered full-time ministry. The sixth died during his senior year in Bible school. The three remaining sons served as district superintendents; one daughter was a pastor's wife, the other a missionary to Latin America and Spain. Ministry, for the Flower family, was a family affair. This was in contrast to E. N. Bell, who married late in life and whose ministry was basically that of an individual.

Second, the Flowers influenced the Assemblies of God through the *Christian Evangel* (now *Today's Pentecostal Evangel*), which they began publishing in 1913.[17] The Flowers gave this magazine to the newly-formed General Council, and it continues to serve as the weekly magazine of the Assemblies of God. Third, it was in the *Pentecostal Evangel* that Alice began publishing the earliest-known weekly Pentecostal Sunday school literature. Sunday school went on to become a significant ministry within the Assemblies of God.

Like Bell, the Flowers were deeply committed to Bible school education as crucial to perpetuating the Pentecostal movement. During her husband's tenure as superintendent of the Eastern District in the early 1930s, Alice began a summer Bible school in Pennsylvania that grew into the present Valley Forge Christian College (Phoenixville, Pennsylvania). J. Roswell himself became a part-time faculty member at several Bible institutes and colleges in the United States and taught short sessions abroad.

Finally, J. Roswell Flower opposed what he viewed as narrow sectarianism; instead, he worked to build bridges between believers with similar faith commitments.[18] Toward that end he labored to make the Assemblies of God a founding member of the National Association of Evangelicals.[19] He also helped to form the Pentecostal Fellowship of North America and the Pentecostal World Fellowship.

Conclusion

The stories of E. N. Bell and J. Roswell and Alice Reynolds Flower provide insight into the social and spiritual lives of early Pentecostals. Perhaps more importantly, they demonstrate how the founders of the Assemblies of God grappled with the movement's inherent tension between charismata and institution. They attempted to create structures that would enhance Pentecostal ministry while protecting the autonomy of the local church and encouraging full devotion to Jesus Christ. The Assemblies of God owes much to these and other pioneers, who laid the spiritual and organizational foundation for its worldwide ministry.

ASSEMBLIES OF GOD

Chairmen:

Eudorus N. Bell
(1914; 1920–1923)

Arch P. Collins
(1914–1915)

John W. Welch
(1915–1920; 1923–1925)

General Superintendents:

William T. Gaston
(1925–1929)

Ernest S. Williams
(1929–1949)

Wesley R. Steelberg
(1949–1952)

Gayle F. Lewis
(1952–1953)

Ralph M. Riggs
(1953–1959)

Thomas F. Zimmerman
(1959–1985)

G. Raymond Carlson
(1986-1993)

Thomas E. Trask
(1993-2007)

George O. Wood
(2007 to present)

Authors:

Darrin Rodgers
Director
Flower Pentecostal Heritage Center

David Ringer
History Professor,
College of the Ozarks

CHAPTER 2

Association
of Vineyard Churches

VINEYARD USA™
A COMMUNITY OF CHURCHES

FOUNDERS:

Kenn Gulliksen

John Wimber

AN ORDINARY MAN SERVING AN EXTRAORDINARY GOD:
John Wimber

By Doug Anderson

The first Vineyard Church started in the '70s when Kenn Gulliksen brought together two Bible studies, both meeting at the houses of singer/songwriters Larry Norman and Chuck Girard. These Bible studies, and others like them, were attended by many popular actors/actresses and musicians, including Bob Dylan. Kenn Gulliksen soon founded several churches, which became known as The Vineyard. Kenn turned the movement over to John Wimber in 1982.

John became a force for worldwide church renewal. He was converted from, in his words, "the pagan pool." In his late 20s, while arranging music and playing with the Righteous Brothers, the musical duo in Las Vegas, John was launched on his spiritual journey. He began to pray and discovered that "God has a book out" (the Bible). Back in Southern California, with his wife, Carol, he joined a small Bible study led by Gunner Payne. One night Carol fell to her knees and accepted Jesus into her life. Weeping, John followed suit.

A sign on a sandwich board carried in downtown Los Angeles had haunted John for years: "I'm a fool for Christ, whose fool are you?" He resolved to be Christ's "fool" and in the next years led hundreds of his friends to Christ. Soon after, he also spoke in tongues but his circle quickly "corrected" him: "This is not God," they said.

When his son was severely bitten by red ants, John carried him home and prayed for his healing. God answered miraculously. Although John was in a cessationist evangelical church (Quaker), these early experiences pointed prophetically to his future.

After attending a Sunday service he asked a friend, "When do we get to do the stuff?" (He meant, "When do we get to do what Jesus did while He was on earth – heal the sick and cast out demons?") His friend replied, "Oh, we don't do it, we just talk about it."

Somewhere in John the resolve grew to do it rather than just talk about it. Later he joined the Institute of Evangelism and Church Growth, associated with Fuller Theological Seminary, where he consulted with hundreds of congregations.

Meanwhile, a remnant from the Friends (Quaker) church began to meet at the Wimbers' home on Sundays. To accommodate the crowd, Carol moved their furniture out onto the lawn. They sang songs to the Lord and prayed for the broken among them. As this fellowship grew, God said to John, "I've seen your ministry, now I'm going to show you mine."

Later John agreed to meet a woman who had a "word from the Lord" for him. He waited impatiently as she simply wept. Exasperated, John finally asked, "So, what's the word?" She replied, "That's it." John felt like someone had hit him in the gut as he heard Jesus in her tears weeping over him.

John began to pastor the large house gathering as it formed a church. God told him to teach his congregation to heal the sick. According to John, not only was no one healed during these early months, but the prayer team caught the colds of those for whom they prayed. Then one Monday morning, a member asked John to pray for his flu-wracked wife. Simply out of obedience, John arrived and prayed perfunctorily. Turning to her husband to explain that God doesn't always heal people, he suddenly realized the woman was out of bed, running off to dress and cook breakfast for him. As he returned to his car he exploded, "We got one!"

Healings began in earnest and word got out. Well-known author Francis MacNutt said, "If you want to start a worldwide movement, just go and heal a few people." This was to be John's experience. Power healing and power evangelism released an apostolic model for church growth.

One Sunday night, at what is now the Anaheim Vineyard, a young evangelist from the days of the Jesus Movement, Lonnie Frisbee, led the service. He announced that the Holy Spirit had been grieved with the Church, "but He is getting over it." He then prayed for the Spirit to come. Suddenly hundreds of people were on the floor, "out" in the power of the Spirit, many chattering in tongues. Carol Wimber was delighted. John was perplexed. *Was this right?*

The next morning a fellow pastor called, "I don't know what this means, but the Lord wants me to tell you, 'It's Me, John.'"

Within months hundreds of young people were converted, baptized, and sharing their faith. John taught them, "The meat [of the Word] is on the street [doin' the stuff]."

Worship was central to the Anaheim Vineyard. As a professional musician, John began to write new music, leading his worship team from the keyboard. This included high praise and intimate love songs to Jesus, sung uninterrupted for a half hour. The musicians were understated. John didn't provide overhead lyrics. Rather than singing about God, they sang to God. "I love the Lord" became "I love You, Lord." John taught that the congregation is the choir. We all sing before "an Audience of One." John's Vineyard worship would go worldwide and provoke a dramatic change in renewed and mainline churches. No longer was worship a warm-up for the sermon. Worship was an end in itself. Moreover, John experienced that as worship ascends, the Spirit descends with people converted or healed on the spot.

At Fuller Theological Seminary in Pasadena, California, returning missionaries and leaders from developing countries reported miracles, healings, and deliverance from demons as a regular part of their ministry, but they needed a theological grid for this. In response, what was then called "School of World Mission" organized a class, MC 510: "Signs, Wonders, and Church Growth." John shared in the teaching, along with Professor Peter Wagner. By the early 1980s it became the largest class in the history of the seminary.

After the lectures students stayed for an optional clinic, where they practiced what had been taught. Many, including some faculty, were empowered by the Spirit, experienced the release of spiritual gifts, and received their own healing.

Fuller exposed John to the New Testament theology of George Ladd. For him, Jesus not only preached the in-breaking of the kingdom of God but also manifested it through healing the sick, casting out demons, forgiving sins, and even raising the dead. This warred against Satan's dark counter-kingdom, restored God's fallen creation, and anticipated Jesus' final victory, consummating the Kingdom in His glorious return.

Ladd taught that the Church ministers in the tension between the "already" and the "not yet." In the "already" we see the Spirit poured out, the sick healed, and the dead raised (although John never saw a dead person come back to life). In the "not yet" there is no final perfect healing or restoration now. This happens only when Jesus returns. Ladd provided the theological grid John needed. Kingdom theology became foundational for all he did in healing, spiritual warfare, community building, and evangelism. This brought radical renewal to the church and radical power (in healing and evangelism) to the world as the church "did the stuff." John's impact on the Church of England was so historic that the (London) *Times* editorialized against the "Wimberites" who were undermining its traditionalism. (At John's memorial service, Bishop David Pytchis would comment that no one had had a greater impact on the church there since John Wesley.)

John then took his "Signs and Wonders" class worldwide in seminars attended by thousands. He never saw himself as a lone healing evangelist or apostle. His passion was to equip the whole Church for Kingdom ministry. As he put it, "Everybody gets to play."

John wanted the Church to get out of the grandstands, where it cheers the professionals on, and onto the field. Leaders were to be "player coaches," equipping all the saints for the work of ministry

(Ephesians 4). This led to major renewals of existing churches in the U.S., Canada, South Africa, Australia, and the United Kingdom, and spread from there to Europe, Southeast Asia, and Latin America.

At the same time, John knew that the best way to evangelize was to plant churches. The Vineyard understood itself to be a church planting movement. John's early disciples, such as Todd Hunter, who later led the Vineyard, packed their cars and pioneered the work. Today (2008) there are over 600 Vineyards in the U.S. and scores more on the way. John resisted the pressure to plant overseas, not wanting to compete with existing churches, although God released him later to do so. Today there are ten International Associations of Vineyard Churches outside the United States, consisting of over 700 local congregations. How then can we sum up John's contributions to the Pentecostal/Charismatic Movement?

First, although in the same stream, John wanted to be known neither as a Pentecostal or charismatic. He agreed with Peter Wagner that the Vineyard was a part of the "Third Wave." The Church must experience God-centered worship, the teaching of God's Word, and Jesus' works released in a Spirit-filled "ministry time." This included invitations for salvation, healing, filling of the Spirit, and a welcome of "words of knowledge" with current prophetic direction. John was significantly gifted in this area.

While teaching at Fuller, God suspended this gifting in John for a season. John grew desperate, crying out to the Lord. Then, when a member of Fuller's board visited his class, the Lord restored the gift and gave John a score of words for her in just a couple of minutes. Nevertheless, he wanted the Vineyard to be "naturally supernatural." He avoided temptations of hype or overstatement. John would let ministry be released, saying, "Let the bush grow, we can trim it back later." He spelled faith "r – i – s – k." A pioneer risk taker, this man of faith was an object of regular and, at times, vindictive attacks from those who opposed him.

Second, John anticipated the "post-modern," "post-Enlightenment" period. He was never trapped by rationalism. In fact,

John was essentially "pre-modern." He identified with the miraculous moves of the Spirit throughout Church history. One of his favorite books was written by the first British historian, the Venerable Bede, on the life of St. Cuthbert, who lived in the seventh century. John's life paralleled Cuthbert's in many ways: prophetically driven, filled with the Spirit, operating in the miraculous, and evangelizing the pagan world of his time.

Third, John was committed to both the Word and Spirit. Holding to absolute biblical authority, he measured all supernatural events, prophetic words, and ministry activities by the Scriptures. When a parishioner who feared manifestations of the Spirit asked, "How far is this going to go?" John held up a Bible and replied, "No further than this." He joked later that his response was not as safe as that man thought. John interpreted the Bible from the vantage point of historical exegesis and evangelical faith. He avoided the excesses of allegory, and, at the same time, heard God speak currently with a "living word" through his devotional use of Scripture. However, he viewed mainline churches as "pneumatically deficient."

Intimacy with God was the heart-theme of his life's journey. The road led through worship, obedience, and surrender to the Spirit. Submission to biblical authority and the ministry of the Spirit lived in creative tension for John. He called his followers to "see what the Father is doing" and "hear what the Spirit is saying" and enter into it. He would change course in a sermon because, "God told me to do so." He would wait for direction from the Spirit as he entered into ministry time, praying for the sick.

Fourth, John called the Church to compassion. This empowered his healing ministry. He constantly gave away his resources saying, "Whatever God has given me, I want to give to you." He started one of the largest relief ministries in Southern California. His church in Anaheim served a million meals each year on site and built a huge food bank to care for the poor and homeless. He insisted that Kingdom ministry must be directed to the dispossessed. This humble servant poured himself out with great cost to his wife, his family, his energy, and eventually his health as he battled cancer and died of a concussion in 1997.

Fifth, John was Spirit-driven. The presence of the Kingdom meant that the Church must be empowered and gifted for ministry. He taught that the filling of the Spirit (which John preferred over the "baptism of the Spirit") was experiential and that the gifts of the Spirit were available to all situationally, like tools in a toolbox, for ministry. The future aspect of the Kingdom explained why all who were evangelized were not converted and why all who were prayed for were not healed. Abandoning triumphalism and its roots in Wesleyan holiness teaching, Wimber moved the Vineyard into "faith healing" based on the tensions built into Kingdom come and coming. He never taught that faith could force God's hand. Citing John's gospel, he said we are to see what the Father is doing, participate, and "bless" it. God initiates and we respond.

Sixth, John, at heart, was an evangelist. He wanted his churches to be "naturally supernatural" and "culturally current." John often wore a Hawaiian sport shirt on the platform. He adopted non-religious language. He was always aware of communicating to the "pagan pool" from which he came. As people came to Christ they needed to be nurtured in the faith. This demanded weekly small "Kinship" groups which held the key to pastoring and discipleship. He taught his leaders to grow the Church from the inside out. As people commit to relationships and ministry, lasting Church growth takes place.

John Wimber would be embarrassed to be counted among the great leaders of the Church. He described himself as spare change in the Lord's pocket to be spent as He wills. Often he would remark, "I'm just a fat man trying to get to heaven." This self-depreciation was never intended to contradict salvation as total grace and total gift. It simply showed that John's ministry was not to be showcased. He never took himself that seriously. He did take Christ totally seriously and poured out his life for Him. Like a stone dropped into a pool, the ripples continue to this day.

ASSOCIATION OF VINEYARD CHURCHES

National Director & Presidents:

Todd Hunter
(1997-2000)

Berten A. Waggoner
(2000 to present)

Author:

Doug Anderson
National Coordinator, Vineyard USA

CHAPTER 3

Canadian
Assemblies *of* God

(formerly The Italian Pentecostal Church of Canada)

FOUNDERS:

Carlo Pavia

Luigi Ippolito   Ferdinando Zaffuto

ZAFFUTO, PAVIA, AND IPPOLITO:
Seekers of Truth

By Daniel Ippolito

When the Pentecostal revival swept across Canada at the beginning of the twentieth century, the pioneers of the Italian Pentecostal Church of Canada were new immigrants to Canada in search of a better life. These young immigrants were not theologians, scholars, or men of wealth. They lacked Bible college training, church doctrine and government, and religious experience or practices. Yet today, we are witnesses of the great work God was pleased to do through them by His Holy Spirit. God blessed them far beyond their imaginations.

The Italian Pentecostal Church of Canada (IPCC) marked its humble beginnings in the city of Hamilton, in the province of Ontario, Canada, when eight men and their families who attended a Mission of the Italian Presbyterian Church left to open a storefront mission of their own, which they called the Chiesa Cristiana Italiana Indipendente. Three men of this Independent Italian Christian Church, all from Sicily, Italy, became the early pioneers: Ferdinando Zaffuto, Carlo Pavia, and Luigi Ippolito.

Ferdinando Zaffuto was born March 6, 1882. A self-taught man with little public education, Ferdinando came to Canada to work as a butcher. In one of his brief writings, Ferdinando said that in 1909 he received a little gospel light (probably referring to the Italian Presbyterian Mission). Nonetheless, in 1913, when he came in contact with Pentecostals, he was converted, baptized in water, and received the baptism of the Holy Spirit.[1] He married Concettina Pavia in January of 1908, reared a family, ministered for some 51 years, and went home to be with the Lord February 2, 1966, at the age of 84.

A man of faith, Ferdinando left his secular work and devoted himself wholly to the work of the Lord when he heard God's call to the ministry. In those early days there was no pastoral financial support, but Ferdinando trusted God for the needs of his family. God honored his faith and faithfulness.

Carlo Pavia, Ferdinando's brother-in-law, was the same age, better educated and known to be a man of prayer, gentleness, and humility. He became recognized as a leader among the group of eight for several years.

Luigi Ippolito, born May 25, 1891, was a shoemaker by trade. His relatives in Hamilton sent him money to go to Canada. In September of 1909, he left Palermo, Italy, in the company of an older cousin who had already been to Canada. When they arrived at Naples, Luigi fell gravely ill and was unable to eat or drink. When the ship landed at New York's famous Ellis Island after 14 days at sea, Luigi was taken to the hospital, suspected of having tuberculosis. Upon his arrival in Hamilton, Luigi's cousin reported the incident to his relatives, who immediately sent Luigi money to obtain the help of an immigration lawyer. Still, Luigi was told he would absolutely have to return to Italy on the next ship. From his hospital room, Luigi watched the ships come and go until November 1, when he was called to the immigration court.

His relatives finally found Pietro Giamanco, a New York businessman and property owner who would appear in court that day on behalf of Luigi. The judge asked Pietro if he knew what it meant to take full responsibility for Luigi. He replied he was ready and willing to do so. Then the judge inquired as to his financial status. Pietro replied by stating he was the owner of some stores in New York, and was in possession of $40,000. When the judge called Luigi's name Luigi stood, believing he was being called before the judge. The judge asked Pietro if he recognized Luigi, and seeing Luigi on his feet, Pietro signaled with his hand to Luigi. Actually, Luigi did not understand a word in English and the two gentlemen did not know each other. Nonetheless Luigi was called before the judge, given all of his official entry papers, and declared free to go with Mr. Giamanco.

Pietro took the papers in one hand and Luigi's hand in the other, and together they left the courtroom. Luigi considered this to be a miracle from God, because God knew what the future had in store for him. The kind businessman treated Luigi to a meal at a local restaurant and then put him on a train for Hamilton, Ontario, Canada. There Luigi was reunited with his relatives. He often recalled that courtroom scene, how a stranger rescued him and allowed him to begin a new life.

Soon after his arrival in Hamilton, Luigi's friends introduced him to the Presbyterian Church Italian Mission, which Luigi attended for three years. His friends, though, had been under the ministry of an "old evangelist of the true salvation" and they had felt something from the Lord. They asked their new pastor if they could meet in a small room of the church to have prayer before his message on Sunday morning. When the pastor vigorously opposed the idea, the little group, along with Luigi, decided to leave the mission. In 1912 they collected eighty dollars and opened the Independent Italian Christian Church, a storefront mission. Someone from the group would bring the message on Sunday – usually Carlo (Charles) Pavia, who, according to Luigi, would speak while smoking his pipe. He was a godly man, though, dedicated to the Lord and to prayer.

In June 1913 these "seekers after truth" of the Italian mission came in contact with English-speaking Pentecostal brethren holding revival services nearby. During a time of prayer, two visitors entered the storefront mission and lifted their voice in prayer, moving the hearts of those present. One of these two brethren was remembered as Brother Marshall of Hamilton. The other was a Jewish evangelist from the USA, who was remembered as Brother Cohen. When these two invited the Italian brethren to their revival services, the brethren not only attended, but joined these believers of the Pentecostal faith.

Soon after joining the Pentecostal believers, Luigi and a close friend went to a meeting and witnessed the Holy Spirit move in a manner they had never seen before. A person seated in front of them had such an extraordinary joyful experience that Luigi's friend attempted to calm him down. When Luigi's friend extended his arms toward the man, the Spirit of the Lord began to move upon the friend, and he, too, became filled with joy.

On July 13, 1913, in a service in the Pentecostal mission, thirteen believers received the baptism of the Holy Spirit. Of these, two were Canadian and the other eleven were Italian.[2] They soon realized their experience was the same as that recorded in the book of Acts on the day of Pentecost. These Italian converts confessed their faith in Christ in water baptism by immersion in Lake Ontario. Luigi also received the baptism of the Holy Spirit. Shortly after, God called him to the ministry. He married Mary Piedmonte of Holley, New York, in 1917, reared a family, and ministered for some 51 years until he went to be with the Lord November 8, 1965. During the course of his long and faithful ministry the courtroom scene never faded from his memory. He realized God had a purpose for his life.

Soon after the opening of the mission, two leaders from the Assemblea Cristiana (Italian Pentecostal Church) of Chicago, where God had poured out His Spirit among Italians in 1907, came to visit the newly formed church of Hamilton (1913-1914). One was John Perrou, a young, powerful preacher full of faith and of the Holy Spirit; the other was Agostino Lencioni, an older, recognized leader in the church of Chicago. Agostino helped set the church in order, naming Carlo Pavia as elder and Ferdinando Zaffuto as a deacon. When these two leaders engaged in visitation outside of Hamilton, they appointed Luigi Ippolito as elder.[3]

The lives of Carlo Pavia, Ferdinando Zaffuto, and Luigi Ippolito were radically changed by the powerful Word of God and the Holy

Spirit. The Holy Spirit quickened their spirits and gave them a holy boldness to witness to relatives, friends, and all they would meet. Their preaching was plain and simple, but they preached with power, conviction, and the anointing of God's Spirit.

After establishing the mission in Hamilton and seeing souls saved and filled with the Spirit, in 1914 Carlo Pavia and Ferdinando Zaffuto visited Toronto, about 40 miles away, to preach the gospel to Italians. They located Toronto's "little Italy" and went from house to house witnessing of their newfound faith.[4] In 1915 Brother Zaffuto took up residence in Toronto so he could preach to the Italians in this city.

On one occasion Ferdinando was invited to preach in an Italian Methodist church in Toronto. When one of the new immigrants, Felix LiSanti, heard Ferdinando preach, Felix experienced a remarkable conversion. Another immigrant, Luke DiMarco, also converted at this time. These two became leaders in the Toronto church and began to witness to their families, friends, and fellow countrymen. In less than two months the number of those saved rose to 25, mostly young men. Nearly all were soon baptized in the Holy Spirit.[5]

One of the early converts offered two rooms in his home as a meeting place. Before long that house was full. The group rented a building in downtown Toronto at the corner of Bay (formerly Terrauley) and Gerrard Streets. Worship took place on the ground floor. Several families of believers lived in the rented quarters on the second and third floors.[6] From 1915 to 1917 Luke DiMarco provided the leadership for these meetings, along with Carlo Pavia, Felix LiSanti, and Donato Fontanarosa.[7]

From 1914 to 1916 the leaders from Hamilton assisted regularly in the establishing of the Toronto church. In September 1917, Ferdinando Zaffuto became its first pastor.[8] About this time one of the first pioneers, Carlo Pavia, left the brethren to join another movement, but not before the Toronto church became the center for evangelism for Ontario and Quebec.

In early April of 1919, when the work in Toronto was growing,

Ferdinando called Luigi Ippolito, who was pastoring in the first Italian church in Hamilton, to come and help with the growing work. For a year both men worked together. Then Brother Zaffuto returned to pastor the church of Hamilton and Brother Ippolito left to minister in New York City. Two leaders were appointed, Donato Fontanarosa and Felix LiSanti. After his brief visit to the United States, Brother Ippolito returned to Toronto and took over the leadership of the church. Under his leadership, the congregation grew in number and was incorporated under the name "Assemblea Cristiana."

Luigi Ippolito reared his family in Toronto and served as pastor for almost 40 years. He supported himself and his family by his trade as a shoemaker. He gladly and faithfully pastored the church, receiving no financial support. Both Brothers Zaffuto and Ippolito looked forward "with respect unto the recompense of the reward" (Hebrews 11:26).

In 1927, a second church was opened in the Italian community, with Luigi Ippolito as pastor. Ferdinando Zaffuto returned from Hamilton to pastor the first church he had left in 1920. In 1944 the two churches came together and both Ferdinando and Luigi ministered together for several years. At the end of World War II, the doors of immigration were opened and a number of believers came to Toronto from Italy. Many were responding to the gospel message and being saved. In 1956 it became necessary to expand into two churches, Pastor Zaffuto pastoring one church and Pastor Ippolito the other.

During this time of revival, brethren carried the gospel to Italians in other parts of Canada and more churches were established.

In the early days there was a close fellowship among pastors and churches but no organization. In 1944 the early leaders called for a conference in Toronto to form a cooperative fellowship. In 1945 the conference adopted the name, The Christian Church of North America, though the name was not accepted by the government for incorporation. In 1958, the General Conference passed a resolution for the fellowship of churches to apply for incorporation in Quebec under the name The Italian Pentecostal Church of Canada, which was granted by the government on October 29, 1959. Luigi Ippolito was elected as General Superintendent and served until he went home to be with the Lord in 1965.

A final word in praise of our early pioneers: The Old Testament Prophets were called "seers," no doubt because they could see what others could not see and could look ahead concerning God's purposes and plans. I.P.P.C.'s early leaders made provision to offer Sunday school, young people's services, and other special services in English as soon as children and young people became a part of the church. Today, English is the predominant language in its churches.

The early pioneers and believers of the first generation have been promoted to glory and the wave of immigrants from Italy has ceased. The mission of our fellowship remains: to reach out to all men everywhere with the glorious gospel of our Lord and Savior Jesus Christ; regardless of language, nationality, or race. With the new millennium came the realization that the time had come for a change of name. In 2002 the General Conference passed a resolution that The Italian Pentecostal Church of Canada should adopt a new name. By authority of the Government of Canada, a federal charter was granted under the new name: General Conference of the Canadian Assemblies of God; and in the French speaking Province of Quebec, "Conference Generale des Assemblees de Dieu Canadienne."

The Canadian Assemblies of God

Superintendents:

Rev. Luigi Ippolito
(1958-1965)

Alberico DeVito
(1965-1970; 1984-1994)

Antonio DiBiase
(1970-1972)

Daniel Ippolito
(1972-1984; 1994-2002)

David Mortelliti
(2002-2008)

Elio Marrocco
(2008 to present)

Author:

Daniel Ippolito

CHAPTER 4

Church *of* God (Cleveland)

FOUNDERS:

Richard Spurling   R. G. Spurling   William F. Bryant

FAITHFUL PILGRIMS:
Establishing the Church of God

by David G. Roebuck

The eleventh chapter of Hebrews is a vivid reminder that at certain moments in history God calls people to leave the familiar and journey toward an unknown place He is preparing. Along the way those following His leading often endure persecution and suffering. No less can be said for the founders of the Church of God (Cleveland, Tennessee), whose greatest desire was to be God's Church in the last days. For Church of God founders, following God included leaving their former churches and embarking on a spiritual journey into a fresh outpouring and work of the Holy Spirit.

Like others of their time, Church of God founders desired to restore the doctrine and practices of the New Testament church, to live holy lives, and to walk in the power of the Spirit. God honored their faithfulness with a call to holiness, with spiritual empowerment, and with signs and wonders. Richard Green Spurling and William Franklin Bryant were vital to the birth and growth of the Church of God.

Restoring a New Testament Church

The Church of God began in the latter years of the nineteenth century with the ministries of father and son, Richard Spurling and Richard Green Spurling, who was known as "R. G." The Spurlings were Baptists living in the Unicoi Mountains of East Tennessee. While preaching and planting churches, they built and operated grist and lumber mills in the region around Monroe County.

The younger Spurling was a licensed preacher with the nearby Pleasant Hill Baptist Church in Cherokee County, North Carolina; however, he experienced growing discord with the Landmark Baptist movement that dominated the congregations of that region. Believing that human creeds were never infallible and too often led to divisions among Christians, R. G. emphasized the New Testament over creeds. Using the familiar language of the railroad, he described the biblical commands to love God and neighbor as the two golden rails along which God's Church should travel. For R. G., the Landmark Baptist movement had followed the all too typical practice of replacing the golden rails with a narrow creed. Traveling along narrow gauge rails, they limited God's work in the world.

According to R. G. Spurling's testimony, "Having felt it my duty to read my Bible in search of the truth, I soon found myself, so to speak, trying to run a broad gauge engine on a narrow gauge railway." When R. G. refused to limit his ministry to Landmark Baptist congregations, he faced opposition: "They demanded my license, which I readily gave up, hoping that I could preach what I saw the Bible to teach instead of what some other man believed. I preached when impressed to do so and I was again called to account for disobeying their rules. Now I must forever quit preaching or leave my church, so I left them, choosing to obey God rather than man. I was turned out of what I once thought was Christ's only true church."

Excluded from his church, R. G. began a two-year journey of prayer and study to discern his place of ministry. He was soon convinced that the Church needed reformation, and on August 19, 1886, he called for that reformation. R. G.'s invitation revealed the heart of what he believed to be a New Testament model of a local church: "As many Christians as are here present that are desirous to be free from all man-made creeds and traditions, and are willing to take the New Testament, or law of Christ as your only rule of faith and practice; giving each other equal rights and privilege to read and interpret for yourselves as your conscience may dictate, and are willing to sit together as the church of God to transact business as the same come forward."

Eight persons responded to the young preacher's call. Under the authority of his father, Richard, who was an ordained minister, those eight organized a local congregation known as Christian Union. The next month they called R. G. Spurling as their pastor. During the following years R. G. established other Christian Union congregations in Tennessee.

Spurling's efforts might never have resulted in more than a few local congregations in the Unicoi Mountains except that God sent revival. It came in the form of a call to Christian holiness in the nearby North Carolina community of Camp Creek. In the spring of 1886, four evangelists preached a ten-day meeting in the local Shearer schoolhouse. The evangelists proclaimed the necessity of holiness and challenged their hearers to seek sanctification. They were "given to much prayer and fasting," preached earnestly, and throngs of people responded. Church of God Historian Charles W. Conn wrote, "Almost from the start of the meeting, the altars were filled with repentant sinners and seekers for the experience of sanctification. Many skeptics of holiness were convinced, and many more rough-living sinners were converted."

William Franklin Bryant was among those seeking sanctification. He had already been conducting home Bible studies and worship services because the Liberty Baptist Church he attended met only one Sunday a month. He later reported, "At the time I was a member of the Baptist church and none of us believed in sanctification, although I attended this revival. I noticed how those who claimed sanctification would go to their fellowmen and fix everything right…."

Attracted by the changed lives he witnessed, William began to seek the experience himself. He testified about this spiritual pilgrimage, "The spirit within me would cry out, 'Give me the blessing like those other few have received.' Oh, how I had to consecrate my life, dying out to my own selfish nature and forsaking wife and children, father and mother and all my earthly friends and giving up my Baptist church, in fact, making a clean breast of everything. But, thank God, when I got all on the altar, one Thursday morning, about 9:00, I was sanctified while sitting in my saddle on my horse."

When the revival concluded, William continued Sunday school and prayer meetings in the school and in local homes. During those meetings seekers experienced an unexpected outpouring of the Holy Spirit. William later recounted, "The people earnestly sought God, and the interest increased. In one of our prayer meetings, the Holy Ghost began to fall upon the humble, sincere, sanctified believers. While that meeting was in progress, one after another fell prostrate under the power of God and soon quite a number came through speaking in other tongues as the Sprit gave the utterance. The news spread like wildfire, and people came for miles to hear and see the manifestations of the presence of God."

The Spirit of God transformed their lives. Yet, because there are no known documents from that time, we do not have a complete record of what God was doing. Historian Conn wrote that it would be some time later before they "would understand the doctrine, person and nature of the Holy Spirit."

Enduring Persecution

Empowered by the Spirit and preaching what Baptists considered the modern theory of sanctification, the Camp Creek believers began to face severe persecution from their churches and neighbors. According to William Bryant, "The persecutions came from the formal churches that claimed they could not live without sin. This persecution grew until it became dangerous for a true baptized child of God to be caught out alone…. As we taught and preached, the persecutions grew hotter and hotter and the power fell the more."

The holiness believers faced investigation and church discipline. One committee considered the possibility that William might have "hypnotic powers." Another came to his home demanding that he stop holding meetings. Local pastors warned them to cease preaching. Despite these threats William and others refused to keep silent, so their churches excluded them for disobedience and "teaching and harboring erroneous doctrines."

When intimidation and church discipline did not hinder the new movement, opposition turned violent with malicious attempts to disrupt their daily lives as well as their worship services. Opponents poured kerosene into the Bryants' spring, and, on another occasion overturned a barrel of syrup on his porch.

He recalled, "Forming their crowds they would come into our services and raise all sorts of disturbances, and stand in the yard and shoot their guns, whooping and yelling like wild men."

Over time the violence became more dangerous. One man was beaten and bullets were fired into their services. During one assault four shotgun pellets wounded William.

The attacks included attempts to destroy the meeting houses with dynamite and arson. When a mob of 106, including community leaders, openly tore down the church and burned the logs, the holiness believers turned to legal authorities for protection. Although opposition continued, this public act of destruction proved too much for the community to tolerate. It is likely that the persecutors would have been jailed, but William Bryant pleaded for mercy. For him, a spiritual response to such violence was an important aspect of his public testimony. He remembered, "We lay on our faces and cried to God to keep us sweet and let us do nothing to grieve the Holy Ghost. There [were] a number who would hazard their lives for this wonderful Spirit we had, so we asked for the signs to follow us more and more."

Experiencing Signs and Wonders

In addition to speaking in tongues, the Camp Creek believers discovered that miracles and healings accompanied their ministries. Two significant accounts highlight what God was doing in their midst.

One night the Spirit woke William Bryant at 2:00 a.m., and he agonized in prayer until morning. Sitting at the breakfast table unable to eat, he heard a knock on his door. The visitor, "a dear sinner friend," related that his brother lay sick with typhoid fever and desperately needed prayer. William quickly traveled the four miles to where the man lived. When he arrived, the sick brother exclaimed from his bed, "Mr. Bryant, I have been begging Mother to send for you ever since two o'clock this morning. I am a sinner and I don't want to die in my sins and go to hell. I told her if I could get you, the Lord would heal me."

William and the others prayed. He later testified, "The Holy Ghost fell upon me. We rebuked the fever in the name of Jesus Christ and laid our hands upon him and anointed him with oil. This poor man sprang up in the bed screaming at the top of his voice, saying 'Oh, Mother, Mother, God has healed me and saved my soul.'" For William this miracle of salvation and healing was a God-given sign to their persecutors. Instead of malice and retaliation, the sanctified, Spirit-filled believers offered their enemies hope and assurance that the power of God would change lives.

Sometime later R. G. Spurling was preaching in the nearby community of Jones, Georgia. One Sunday evening a desperate father pleaded with R. G. to come pray for his young son, who had been sick for five weeks. The father confided that the doctor had been unable to relieve the boy's sickness. Arriving at the home of this Missionary Baptist family, R. G. was astonished to witness their faith in the Lord's power to heal the boy who was "thin, pale and weak." He attributed this confidence to the fact that another family member had been recently healed.

According to R. G.'s report, "We sang a few songs, prayed a few prayers, during which time I anointed him with oil in the name of the Lord. He had previously been saved, so he was healed and received the baptism with the Holy Ghost and spoke in other tongues. His clothes were put on him and he walked the floor for more than an hour, praising God, talking in tongues and embracing his friends, while the saints that were there shouted and laughed and cried and glorified God for what He had done."

Such healings and Spirit baptisms were common among Church of God members. When reporting this particular testimony, R. G. took the occasion to explain the significance of speaking in tongues. For him, the outpouring of the Spirit and the presence of tongues was clear and certain evidence that the Church was "near the end of the gospel age" and would soon complete her journey in this world. He compared the present-day outpouring of the Holy Spirit with events at the tower of Babel where God had confused their work with unknown tongues. Just as certainly, God was confusing the building of modern human towers, such as nominal churches, with a new outpouring of tongues. Consequently, the building of human monuments would soon come to naught.

R. G. Spurling added the example of Nebuchadnezzar, who had left a great kingdom to his son Belshazzar, but when God broke in with handwriting in an unknown language, the mighty Babylon fell. R. G. surmised, "Now God is speaking again in other tongues to the nominal churches of today and they are rejecting the counsel of God against themselves, not being baptized with the Holy Ghost." Thus for R. G. Spurling and the Church of God, tongues and miracles were both a fresh outpouring of God's blessings and a sign that the Church was "nearing the end of the gospel age."

R. G. concluded his testimony with the biblical image of Abraham's descendents in Egypt preparing to return to the Promised Land. He challenged his readers to view what God was doing as a sign to be prepared for their final journey: "Stand like Israel did on the night of the Passover in Egypt with their shoes on their feet and their staffs in their hands, till Jesus comes." Like Abraham, William Franklin Bryant and R. G. Spurling were on a journey to a "city which has foundations, whose builder and maker is God."

Church of God (Cleveland)

General Overseers:

Ambrose J. Tomlinson
(1909-1923)

Flavius J. Lee
(1923-1928)

Samuel W. Latimer
(1928-1935)

J. Herbert Walker, Sr.
(1935-1944)

John C. Jernigan
(1944-1948)

Hallie L. Chesser
(1948-1952)

Zeno C. Tharp
(1952-1956)

Houston R. Morehead
(1956-1958)

James A. Cross
(1958-1962)

General Overseers:

Wade H. Horton
(1962-1966; 1974-1976)

Charles W. Conn
(1966-1970)

R. Leonard Carroll
(1970-1972)

Ray H. Hughes
(1972-1974; 1978-1982; 1996)

Cecil B. Knight
(1976-1978)

E. Clayton Thomas
(1982-1986)

Raymond E. Crowley
(1986-1990)

R. Lamar Vest
(1990-1994; 2000-2004)

Robert White
(1994-1996)

General Overseers:

Paul L. Walker
(1996-2000)

G. Dennis McGuire
(2004-2008)

Raymond F. Culpepper
(2008 to present)

Author:

David G. Roebuck
Director, Dixon Pentecostal Research Center

CHAPTER 5

Church *of* God *in* Christ

FOUNDER:

C. H. Mason

A MAN SENT FROM GOD:
C. H. Mason

By Leonard Lovett

One of the most monumental figures in American Christianity, Bishop Charles Harrison Mason, was born in 1866, four years after the Emancipation Proclamation. As the founding patriarch of the Church of God in Christ, Bishop Mason's impact radically altered the face of American Christianity.

Bishop Mason was the son of Jerry and Eliza Mason, former slaves and members of the Missionary Baptist Church a few miles from Memphis. Indeed C. H. was one sent from God. As a small child little Charles was stricken with a severe life threatening episode of fever and miraculously healed by the power of God. One year after his father's death (1879) Charles received Christ and was baptized into the Christian faith at the Mount Olive Baptist Church near Plummersville, Arkansas.

After ordination and marriage in 1891, C. H. sought to educate himself by admission to Arkansas Baptist College. By 1894, young Charles had completed his studies. By 1895 the influence of the Holiness Movement, with its emphasis on sanctification, had made an impact on the youthful Mason. Under Wesleyan influence, their message had come to embrace perfection, characterized by "perfect love." A division within the Methodist church in 1880 formed as a result of a controversy over John Wesley's doctrine of sanctification. One group stressed "perfect love" while a separate group stressed a Spirit baptism separate and distinct from conversion.

Sixty-four years earlier (1816) Richard Allen had founded the African Methodist Episcopal Church as a direct result of racial divisions within the Body of Christ on earth. The emphasis on individualism tempered the spirit of the times and set the tone for the rise of black independent churches. Black worship and lifestyle proved to be problematic within mixed fellowships and resulted in the rise of independent black churches. In the midst of religious change and shifting loyalties, Charles Mason became attracted to the Holiness Movement. In 1895 he met Charles Price Jones, a newly elected pastor of the Mt. Helms Baptist Church in Jackson, Mississippi. Charles Jones had been influenced by the doctrine of sanctification as a Baptist pastor in Selma, Alabama. The united preaching of Jones and Mason created a crisis for conservative black Baptist leaders. The preaching of sanctification became so offensive that both preachers were excommunicated from the Baptist denomination.

On the eve of the twentieth century, Jones and Mason participated in an informal group known as "the movement," which consisted of persons from various denominations who embraced the new doctrine of entire sanctification and holiness lifestyle. A loosely organized cluster of small congregations bearing such titles as "Churches of God" and "Churches of Christ" emerged from the movement.

After diligently studying the Scriptures and much prayer and consecration, the search for identity had begun. In 1897, while walking along a street in Little Rock, Arkansas, Elder Mason received the revelation of a name grounded in 1 Thessalonians 2:14 and 2 Thessalonians 1:1, "the churches of God which are in Christ Jesus." During that divine encounter, the denominational name of the largest Pentecostal body in North America was birthed – the Church of God in Christ (COGIC). C. H. Mason remained under the pastorate of Charles P. Jones, who was a gifted poet and hymnologist. The group published *Truth Magazine*, a news periodical. A formal movement had been launched, with Charles

Jones as overseer. Another holiness leader, J. A. Jeter, was placed over Arkansas while C. H. Mason was made overseer of Tennessee, a decision that would prove momentous for future posterity.

Less than a decade later a Pentecostal revival swept Los Angeles, California. In God's providence, William Joseph Seymour (circa, 1870–1922), a Baptist preacher with holiness affiliation, entered the scene. Under the influence of the teaching of Charles Fox Parham, William Seymour was invited to pastor a small holiness mission in Los Angeles. He had been exposed to the message that the baptism in the Holy Spirit is evidenced by speaking in tongues as found in Scripture. That teaching sparked controversy at the holiness mission and William was not invited to return after his first message. Richard and Ruth Asberry opened their arms of love and received William at their home at 216 North Bonnie Brae Street for a Bible study and prayer service. The exuberant worship experience, led by several African-American women, was so crowded the floor caved in from dancing in the Spirit. Soon after, a former African Methodist Episcopal Church, a building that had been converted into a livery stable, became the birthplace of the modern Pentecostal Movement.

William J. Seymour conducted a revival that continued nonstop for three years. Without proper public relations in place, no offerings were received within the worship center for fear it would offend God. Those in search of the move of God came from over 53 nations to receive the baptism in the Holy Spirit. Charles Jones sent C. J. Mason, D. J. Young, and J. A. Jeter during the spring of 1906 to assess the revival that had made every newspaper.

Mason's Baptism in the Holy Spirit

A decade after being baptized in the Holy Spirit, C. H. Mason recalled the following:

> *The first day in the meeting I sat to myself, away from those that went with me. I began to thank God in my heart for all things, for when I heard some speak in tongues, I knew it was*

right though I did not understand it. Nevertheless, it was sweet. I also thanked God for Elder Seymour who came and preached a wonderful sermon. His words were sweet and powerful and it seems that I hear them now while writing. When he closed his sermon, he said, "All of those that want to be sanctified or baptized with the Holy Ghost, go to the upper room; and all those that want to be justified, come to the altar."

I said that is the place for me (the altar), for it may be that I am not converted and if not, God knows it and can convert me. Glory! The second night of prayer I saw a vision. I saw myself standing alone and had a dry roll of paper in my mouth trying to swallow it. Looking up towards the heavens, there appeared a man at my side. I turned my eyes at once, then I awoke and the interpretation came. God had me swallowing the whole book and if I did not turn my eyes to anyone but God and Him only, He would baptize me. I said yes to Him, and at once in the morning when I arose, I could hear a voice in me saying, "I see."

I got a place at the altar and began to thank God. After that, I said, "Lord, if I could only baptize myself, I would do so," for I wanted the baptism so bad I did not know what to do. I said, "Lord, You will have to do the work for me," so I turned it over into His hands. Then I began to ask for the baptism of the Holy Ghost according to Acts 2:41 (KJV): "Then they that gladly received His Word were baptized." Then I saw that I had a right to be glad and not sad.

The enemy said to me, "There may be something wrong with you."

Then a voice spoke to me saying, "If there is anything wrong with you, Christ will find it and take it away and marry you."

Someone said, "Let us sing." I arose and the first song that came to me was "He Brought Me Out (of the miry clay)!" The Spirit came upon the saints and upon me. Then I gave up for the Lord to have His way within me. So there came a wave of glory into me. All of my being was filled with the glory of the Lord. So when He had gotten me straight on my feet, there came a light which enveloped my entire being above the brightness of the sun. When I opened my mouth to say, "Glory!" a flame touched my tongue which ran down me. My language changed and no word could I speak in my own tongue. Oh! I was filled with the glory of the Lord. My soul was then satisfied.

When C. H. Mason returned to share his claim of a third crisis experience (the baptism in the Holy Spirit), he was expelled by Charles Jones and J. A. Jeter. The following year a general assembly was held in Jackson, Mississippi, for the purpose of voting to sever the fellowship of C. H. and his followers, while a general assembly was held simultaneously in Memphis to choose a chief apostle. C. H. Mason was unanimously chosen as chief apostle of the Church of God in Christ, a position he held until his demise November 17, 1961.

God anointed Bishop C. H. Mason to evangelize North America and beyond. Elder D. J. Young was appointed editor of the new periodical, *The Whole Truth*. Bishop Mason ordained ministers across racial lines during one of the most racist periods in our history, just past the turn of the century, and he honored the "prayer tradition" within the black religious experience. His evangelistic endeavors ran counter to mainstream religion and brought him under religious persecution. A converted cotton gin warehouse became a sanctuary of praise.

The revivals in Lexington, Mississippi, became so intense that gunshots were fired into the worship auditorium. C. H. Mason's commitment to the preaching of Hebrews 12:14 (KJV), which says, "Follow peace with all men, and holiness, without which no man shall see the Lord," drew the ire of the Federal Bureau of Investigations for containing anti-war rhetoric. The government tried to build a case against C. H. for fraud and conspiracy. When federal agents confiscated his briefcase for what they thought would be incriminating evidence, they found only a bottle of anointing oil, a handkerchief, and a Bible. The U.S. District Court in Jackson, Mississippi, could never prosecute a case against him. A "kangaroo court" in Paris, Texas, tried to no avail to convict him. A prosecutor en route to try a case against him in Jackson, Mississippi, was killed in a train incident. A mob in Arkansas tried to interrupt a baptism by using a pistol to intimidate the crowd of worshipers. Each time the pistol was pointed away from Bishop it would fire. He came to better appreciate Isaiah 54:17, "No weapon formed against you shall prosper."

Apostolic Leadership Expands

Leadership has to do with the exercise of influence. Bishop Mason's leadership and authority was grounded in his spirituality and total commitment to God. He gave himself to fasting and prayer for many days and nights. He was stripped bare of all pretense as he sought God. From 1909 to 1914 many white ministers received ordination credentials from C. H. for practical and economic reasons, because COGIC was recognized as a legally incorporated church body. This practice resulted in scores of white congregations bearing the name, Church of God in Christ, a fact often omitted by Pentecostal historians. The prevailing racial and social ethos of the times eventually resulted in the discontinuance of this practice. Elders E. N. Bell and H. A. Goss, co-founders of the Assemblies of God, issued a call in 1914 to convene a general council of all Pentecostal saints and Churches of God in Christ at Hot Springs, Arkansas. The call was directed to white saints only. Bishop Mason preached for the newly formed Assemblies of God in 1914 and maintained fellowship with several white Pentecostal leaders. The mandate of leadership would rest upon the founder and chief apostle throughout his life.

In 1911 C. H. appointed Mother Lizzie Woods Roberson from Omaha, Nebraska, as the first leader of the women's department, based on Jeremiah 9:17–20. Under her leadership, Bible Bands, Sunshine Band, Sewing Circle, and later the Home and Foreign

Missions were founded by women in ministry. She was succeeded by Mother Lillian B. Coffey. The role of women in ministry is under revision as women have begun to chart their destiny within the denomination, not without challenges. The COGIC has experienced phenomenal growth and succeeded in making an impact on the global village. Bishop Mason's legacy has been preserved through his successors.

On November 17, 1961, the sun set for one of the most seminal religious leaders of the twentieth century. Historians for years to come will be delving into the mystery of Bishop Charles Harrison Mason, a man sent by God for our times. He now belongs to the ages but his legacy lives on.

Church of God in Christ

Founder and Chief Apostle:

C. H. Mason
(1907 – 1961)

Bishops:

Ozra T. Jones, Sr.
(1961–1968)

James O. Patterson
(1968–1989)

Louis H. Ford
(1990–1995)

Chandler D. Owens
(1996-2000)

Gilbert E. Patterson
(2000-2007)

Charles E. Blake
(2007 to present)

Author:

Leonard Lovett

CHAPTER 6

Church *of* God *of the* Apostolic Faith

FOUNDERS:

Edwin A. Buckles

Oscar H. Bond

PIONEERING THE CHURCH OF GOD OF THE APOSTOLIC FAITH:
Edwin A. Buckles and Oscar H. Bond

By Martin Monacell

L eaders within the early Pentecostal movement demonstrated a profound ability to integrate both primitive, Holy Spirit inspired fervor and pragmatic, organizational ability. In 1914 James O. McKinzie, Edwin A. Buckles, Oscar H. Bond, and Joseph P. Rhoades, leaders of a small network of Pentecostal churches in the south central states, expressed concern for the pressing need for organization and church government amidst a movement often susceptible to hyper-spiritualized fanaticism. These four men called a meeting at the Cross Roads Mission, near Ozark, Arkansas, to establish The Church of God of the Apostolic Faith (The COGAF).

The churches that formed The COGAF emerged from one of the early revivals that helped to define the Pentecostal movement – the 1901 outpouring at Charles F. Parham's Bethel Bible School in Topeka, Kansas. The COGAF leaders held fast to the Wesleyan belief that "entire sanctification" occurred as a second, definite work of grace subsequent to the initial conversion experience. According to this belief, Christians who had a crisis experience of sanctification were enabled to experience perfect love and to live sinless lives. The Wesleyan (also called Holiness) view of sanctification stood as an important doctrine among the earliest American Pentecostal churches, including Parham's Apostolic Faith Movement, the Church of God (Cleveland, Tennessee), the Church of God in Christ, and the Pentecostal Holiness Church.

However, a debate within Pentecostal circles over the nature of sanctification set in motion a series of events that would lead to the formation of The COGAF. In 1910, Chicago pastor William H. Durham, who was baptized in the Spirit at the Azusa Street Revival in Los Angeles in 1907, began to teach against the Wesleyan view of sanctification. Durham instead argued that sanctification was a process that began at conversion and was completed at death, where believers gradually receive the benefits of Christ's finished work at Calvary. Durham's "finished work" teaching sparked heated controversy within the Pentecostal movement. When the Assemblies of God (AG) convened its first meeting in Hot Springs, Arkansas, in April 1914, the opening address delivered by Mack M. Pinson, entitled "The Finished Work of Calvary," made it clear to advocates of a Wesleyan doctrine of sanctification that their view was not welcome.

The COGAF and its four pioneers stood firmly within the Wesleyan Pentecostal camp. They convened their meeting at the Cross Roads Mission, just months after the AG was formed, because they believed that a new body needed to be formed that held to entire sanctification. While initially there was no clear leader, Buckles quickly emerged as a strong guiding force in the organization. The COGAF established a monthly publication, *The Apostolic Faith Messenger*, and elected Oscar H. Bond as its editor. While not one of the founding members of The COGAF, Bond used his platform as newspaper editor to become one of the most outspoken leaders within the organization.

E. A. Buckles

Edwin Alvie Buckles (1877-1938) served as the first moderator of The COGAF. His previous experience as a sheriff helped prepare him to become the leader of this growing movement. Throughout his life, he remained active in full-time ministry, and also worked as a plumber by trade. When struck by illness later in life, the entrepreneurial pastor became a truck farmer to help support his family.

Raised in a Methodist home, Edwin struggled with his faith and calling early in life. He yearned for something more from God. He recounts, "I was a backslider and had gone deep in sin, but thank God that he reclaimed me on the second Saturday night of March, 1909." He wasted no time and preached the very next night at his local Methodist church. But God had more in store for this eager young Christian. He recounts how God had already begun to teach him "that people had to live above sin in this present world."

Describing his experience of entire sanctification, Edwin writes, "I went to the altar on the fifth night of July ... but did not make my consecration complete until about three o'clock in the afternoon the sixth day of July, and thanks be to God, He came in and sanctified me wholly." Two months later Edwin received the experience of the baptism in the Holy Spirit "with the Bible evidence of speaking in other tongues or languages as the Spirit gives utterance."

Edwin's life was not without pain and hardship. He married his first wife in 1902 but she died five years later. He was on his own with three children: Ruth, a newborn, Claude, two years old, and Earnest, almost four. He was unable to care for all of them, so his parents stepped in to care for Earnest and Claude. Edwin remarried in 1910 to Birdie May Clawson. When Edwin suffered a stroke and was left bedridden, Birdie washed clothes and worked as a cook to support the family. She remained a fully devoted wife until his death on May 15, 1938.

Like other Pentecostals, The COGAF spread its message through the printed word. Buckles proved himself a prolific writer. He authored tracts, a brief history of the movement, and articles for *The Apostolic Faith Messenger*. Even though he struggled with severe health problems late in his life, including several heart attacks and a stroke that paralyzed the left side of his body for a period of time, he remained ever present at The COGAF conference meetings and through writings on such topics as the qualifications of pastors, the state of young people in the church, and tithing.

Buckles' Influence

Like most early Pentecostals, Edwin considered himself a restorationist, presenting The COGAF as the continuation of the early church of the apostles described in the Book of Acts:

> *The question might arise in some people's mind why I say, "The Church of God, of the Apostolic Faith." The reason is a simple one: The Bible name for the church is, "The Church of God;" and I put these words, "of the Apostolic faith," to show that we are teaching, and putting into effect, the doctrines which the apostles taught and practiced. (Acts 2:42): "And they continued steadfastly in the apostles' doctrine and fellowship, and in breaking of bread, and in prayers.*

He proceeded to state that the outpouring of the Spirit beginning with the 1901 Topeka revival continued in perfect accord with the faith of the apostles until 1910 when Durham began to openly teach against sanctification as a second work of grace. According to Edwin's experience and biblical exegesis, a progressive view of sanctification could not be tolerated. One must experience entire sanctification before he or she can receive the baptism in the Holy Spirit.

The organizers of the first meeting of the Assemblies of God in 1914 sent a letter to Edwin inviting him to attend. In this letter he was allegedly told, "Leave your hobby horse at home," which Edwin believed referred to his strong belief in entire sanctification. Feeling put-off by this invitation, Edwin did not attend and later that same year helped to pioneer The COGAF. In the final pages of his brief history of the movement, he goes on the clear offensive against anyone teaching the "finished work of Calvary." For Edwin, entire sanctification was much more than his "hobby horse" – he believed the apostles clearly preached the Wesleyan doctrine and it was an essential part of the Christian life.

Concerning the state of young people in The COGAF, Edwin appeared to be ahead of his time, arguing that the older generation must be careful not to place undue restrictions on the younger generation. He wrote, "Now and then people say, 'The way is too straight for my children to accept.' If so, YOU have made it that way…. We are persuaded that the child with proper training will not despise the way. We may become fanatical and cause our children to despise us, and the way we are in." Edwin also attacked the legalistic attitudes of many Pentecostals, referencing a story about a young married couple who left the church because "some unwise person 'opened fire' on them in testimony about their dress." While many early Pentecostals maintained a stubborn legalism over certain holiness standards, Edwin called for more balance, recognizing that the overzealous fervor of many in the movement was driving away young people who represented the future of the denomination.

Edwin's pragmatic thinking in the midst of an often disorganized and passionate movement remains his legacy. According to former General Superintendent Joe L. Edmonson, The COGAF owed its continued existence to Edwin's leadership. Every movement needs at least one person who consistently stands up as the voice of reason. More often than not, Edwin Buckles answered this call.

O. H. Bond

Oscar Harrison Bond (1889-1957) wielded significant influence in The COGAF as editor of *The Apostolic Faith Messenger*. Oscar was born in what is now Cherokee County, Oklahoma. He married Georgia Capps in 1911 and struggled to support her for most of their early marriage. He desired to be a newspaper editor, but due to financial need, became a second grade teacher instead. In 1914, he suffered a nervous breakdown and began to use morphine intravenously, causing his wife to leave him. That year was the lowest point of his life, but his life was about to change.

Oscar attended an "old-fashioned Holy Ghost revival meeting" on January 1, 1915, where he committed his life to Jesus Christ and was "born again." As the revival progressed, the new Christian received the experience of full sanctification and, several days later, the baptism in the Holy Ghost with the evidence of speaking in other tongues. In reference to his experience of entire sanctification,

Oscar recalled someone at the revival saying, "You can tell he has the blessing." According to Oscar, everything about him changed. He was now fully free of sin and able to "live this good salvation; preach it clean; and stand for God in the face of men and devils!" In late January, Edwin arrived at the revival meeting and baptized Oscar in water.

The subsequent events of Oscar's life proved the reality of his transformation. Later in 1915, his wife returned to him and did not leave his side until his death. Bond began to preach the gospel almost immediately after his conversion experience. In February of 1918, he was ordained as a COGAF minister and immediately became one of its most vocal members. At The COGAF conference on April 2, 1919, in Mulberry, Kansas, Oscar was elected vice president of the organization. His ongoing dream of being a newspaper editor translated into his becoming a persistent advocate to create a denominational publication. He eventually received approval from The COGAF in 1924 to establish *The Apostolic Faith Messenger*. Oscar borrowed $50 from a friend to purchase his first press, a foot powered machine, and other necessary equipment to get started. Financial and organizational setbacks held up publication, but the would-be editor persisted, and in September 1930 he released the first issue.

Bond's Influence

Oscar used his "little paper" as a platform to preach and teach on topics he found especially important. Looking through the issues of *The Apostolic Faith Messenger*, one immediately notices that not only did Oscar edit it; he also wrote much of it. As with Edwin and other leaders in The COGAF, he argued tirelessly for entire sanctification. In one article, he chided those Pentecostals who "will go at great length to set forth the doctrine of the baptism in the Holy Ghost, but who ... divert from the facts as concerns the original plan of salvation – bury in oblivion ... the truth concerning the open biblical doctrine of sanctification as having anything to do with one's getting the real baptism in the Spirit." Interestingly, in his autobiography, Oscar took a much different approach to this issue. Rather than argue from Scripture, he argued from his experience. He wrote, "It [entire sanctification] was real in my life…. A truly sanctified person is not going to fight over doctrinal issues." For many early Pentecostals, including Oscar, doctrine was true not just because it was scriptural, but also because it represented how God truly works among fully devoted Christ-followers.

Whether through his newspaper or on the floor of conference meetings, Oscar was always ready to make his voice heard. For example, at one COGAF conference, he presented a lengthy resolution referring to the "slack" nature of those not in attendance, questioning their dedication to God's work, and challenging them to "fulfill the law of Christ" by attending future meetings. At a conference a few years later, Edwin interrupted Oscar several times as Oscar pontificated on his views regarding the biblical rights of women. While we have no record of the actual comments made by Oscar, and Edwin did later apologize for the interruptions, it seems reasonable to assume that, in typical fashion, Oscar spoke for a lengthy amount of time and used forceful rhetoric.

Oscar was well liked by many during his lifetime, but later COGAF leaders remembered him as a stubborn and legalistic man. In contrast to the pragmatic Edwin, Oscar was often radical and confrontational, writing numerous articles exhorting holiness standards such as appropriate dress and keeping the Sabbath. However, the obituary written by Earnest Buckles, son of Edwin, remembers him fondly as a man who "put his soul, mind, inspiration, and physical effort" into the publication of his newspaper, publishing "the gospel like he preached it," and blessing hundreds in the process. Unfortunately, *The Apostolic Faith Messenger* died with Bond in 1957, a testament to the fact that the paper thrived because of him.

Conclusion

E.A. Buckles and O.H. Bond contributed significantly to the foundation of The Church of God of the Apostolic Faith. Their pragmatic drive and primitive fervor combined to bring many to Christ. At The COGAF Conference in November 2007, Kelly Ward was elected General Superintendent at the young age of 35, a significant statement of affirmation to the next generation of leaders within the fellowship. While The COGAF has remained relatively small, the fellowship has continued to press forward in the mission to which it has been called.

THE CHURCH OF GOD OF THE APOSTOLIC FAITH

General Superintendents:

Edwin A. Buckles
(1914-1937)

P. A. Henegar
(1937-1952)

J. L. Sullivent
(1952-1979)

Joe L. Edmonson
(1979-2007)

Author:

Kelly Ward
(2007 to present)

Martin Monacell

CHAPTER 7

Church *of* God
Mountain Assembly

FOUNDERS:

J. H. Parks

Rev. Steve Bryant

Tom Moses

William Douglas

J. H. PARKS:
Caught up by the Spirit

By James Kilgore

The Church of God Mountain Assembly, like other Pentecostal organizations, is a stream flowing from the great outpouring of the Spirit that began on the Day of Pentecost when the hundred and twenty were filled with the Spirit and began to speak with other tongues as the Spirit gave them utterance. Upon the foundation of the apostles and prophets the Church was built, Jesus Christ being the chief cornerstone (Ephesians 2:20).

In the intervening centuries since Acts 2, great revivals were fanned into flame by the Holy Ghost. In the wake of these revivals the tendency of some was to drift into formalism and depart from the full gospel. Others, however, like those during the closing period of the nineteenth century, and following a wave of intercession initiated by the Spirit, captivated many people from around the world with an increasing cry to God for a fresh Pentecost. Men like J. H. Parks helped spark those revivals.

In 1895 Rev. J. H. Parks, a United Baptist pastor, introduced the doctrine of sanctification to McCreary County, Kentucky. This doctrine caught the attention of three other Baptist pastors in the area: Rev. Steve Bryant, Tom Moses, and William Douglas. These gentlemen began to preach sanctification, living free from sin. They preached under great anointing, and people began to seek a deeper experience with God. Individuals were filled with the Holy Ghost and spoke in tongues. These seekers of God were unaware the Lord was blessing fellow Christians in similar ways across the nation.

Many accepted the doctrine of sanctification, although the leaders of the Baptist Association at that time said men could not live without sin. In 1903 these leaders executed an order in the Baptist Association in McCreary County to exclude from fellowship and call in credentials of all ministers who preached that men could be lost after regeneration.

In 1905 the credentials of Parks, Bryant, Moses, and Douglas were revoked. The charge was clear: they taught "man could be lost after regeneration." After the trial, five Baptist churches left in sympathy with their holiness leaders. One year later, in 1906, they met at Jellico Creek, Kentucky, to organize as "Church of God." On October 11, 1907, the first General Assembly was held at the Jellico Creek Church in Whitley County, Kentucky.

Because of differences in worship, the churches of the new organization were not accepted well in most areas. In the aftermath of rejection, these churches were subject to persecutions, often severe at times. Enemies of the churches pelted the buildings with rocks during services and attacked many of the ministers and saints. The Lord kept His hand of protection upon those who trusted Him.

At one of the meetings where Rev. J. H. Parks was preaching, men came to the church with knives and pistols, intent on breaking up the service. It was reported they threatened to kill Brother Parks. When he got up to preach, he rebuked these men in the name of the Lord, and it is said the Spirit of God lifted him up to the ceiling of the church. The men who had planned to harm him fell down as dead men. Before they left, Rev. Parks' wife, Rachel, who apparently thought the Lord was calling her husband home, cried out, "Lord, don't take him now!"

When this band of God's faithful first formed, they did not use the name "Mountain Assembly." At that time church leaders were unaware of any other organization called "Church of God." After discovering other churches with the same name, however, "Mountain Assembly" was added for distinction in 1911. The organization was never part of another denomination.

Headquarter offices were established at Jellico, Tennessee, where the Church of God Mountain Assembly has continued to expand into several states of the United States and into many foreign countries. The missions department has been engaged in ministry for over 30 years. The youth department has served over 50 years, with the campgrounds in Highland County, Ohio.

CHURCH OF GOD MOUNTAIN ASSEMBLY

Moderator:

S.N. Bryant
(1907-1938)

Moderator/General Overseer:

A.J. Long
(1939-1946)

John H. Bryant
(1946-1947)

Luther Gibson
(1947-1950)

Clayton Lawson
(1950-1960; 1980-1984)

Ira Moses
(1960-1972)

C.B. Ellis, Jr
(1972-1976)

Jerome Walden
(1976-1980)

Kenneth Massingill, Sr.
(1984-1988)

Jasper Walden
(1988-1994)

Cecil Johnson
(1994-2000)

Lonnie Lyke
(2000–2004)

Fred Cornelius
(2004-2006)

Donnie Hill
(2006 to present)

CHAPTER 8

Church *of* God *of* Prophecy

FOUNDER:

Ambrose Jessup Tomlinson

PENTECOSTAL TRANSFORMATION OF A LIFE AND A MOVEMENT:
Ambrose Jessup Tomlinson

By Adrian L. Varlack, Sr.

Since Ambrose Jessup (A. J.) Tomlinson's own dramatic baptism with the Holy Ghost in 1908, the churches he led, Church of God Cleveland, Tennessee, and what became the Church of God of Prophecy also of Cleveland, Tennessee, have continued in the classical Pentecostal tradition.[1] Gaston B. Cashwell, who had his own Pentecost at the Azusa Street outpouring in Los Angeles in late 1906,[2] was invited by A. J. Tomlinson to preach on the Holy Ghost at the third General Assembly of the Church of God, held January 10-12, 1908.[3] Given the holiness background of the church's leadership at the time, it is noteworthy how the program for the Assembly read in expectation of Cashwell:

> **January 11, 1908**
> *7:00 p.m.: Service on Pentecostal lines.*
> *We expect Brother G. B. Cashwell of Dunn, N. C.*
> **January 12, 1908**
> *10:40 a.m.: Preaching or Pentecostal Service*
> *7:00 p.m.: Service on Pentecostal Lines* [4]

A. J. had been preaching about the Holy Ghost from the Book of Acts for some time before he was baptized with the Spirit. He claimed, for instance, that shortly after his very definite sanctification experience (about 1893), he was "hungry for God" and was led in seeking a Pentecostal experience, though with little or no cooperation from others. Some even regarded him as fanatical.[5] In an edited version of his diary, an entry dated October 30, 1897, includes the following sentence:

"Received Holy Ghost about March 1896."[6]

This would have been 12 years before his 1908 experience. Exactly what was meant by his statement, "Received Holy Ghost," given his sanctification experience above, remains unclear.

In A. J.'s greatest literary work, *The Last Great Conflict*, which was written about 1913, he states as follows:

*In January 1907, I became more fully awakened on the subject of receiving the Holy Ghost **as He was poured out on the day of Pentecost**. I did not have the experience, so I was almost always among the seekers at the altar. The Lord gave great revivals, and souls were converted and sanctified, and some really went through and were baptized with the Holy Ghost evidenced by the speaking in tongues [emphasis mine].*[7]

A. J. was a relentless and honest seeker after truth, so we can assume he had some special encounters with the Spirit, but not according to the apostles' experience in Acts 2. Five years after he had been baptized in the Holy Ghost with the evidence of speaking in other tongues, he wrote his thoughts about the difficulties of obtaining God's spiritual blessings. Of course his diary includes numerous early references to his waiting on the Holy Ghost, being led or directed by the Spirit, or that the Spirit worked mightily in various services. This type of language would not have been unusual even for those who remained in the Holiness Movement. The following paragraph seems to be his attempt to systematize by degrees the efforts expended in seeking spiritual experiences:

In God's economy He has made the spiritual blessings difficult to obtain in like proportion. Justification by faith is more easily seen and obtained than sanctification through the blood of Christ. In like manner is the baptism with the Holy Ghost a little deeper down and more difficult to obtain, and much more

patience is required in seeking for it, as is the case with the search
for gold and precious stones. And the result is that many fail to
find the precious experience because so much time, patience and
perseverance is required.[8]

Perhaps this comment reflected his personal, protracted experience of more than a year (1906–1908) seeking the baptism with the evidence of speaking in tongues. One wonders whether this might have been the beginning or at least an embryonic reflection of the three-step approach that developed in the classical Pentecostal altar and in public testimonies during Pentecostal services.[9]

In the late nineteenth century, regardless of the common talk among holiness believers of being led by the Spirit or being filled with the Spirit, there seemed to be that lingering sense that there was always "something more." For A. J. Tomlinson, the defining moment that terminated his search and settled the issue of a true Pentecostal experience, once for all, was Sunday morning, January 12, 1908. While listening to Gaston Cashwell's sermon, A. J. had a very dramatic and physical encounter with the Holy Ghost. His descriptions are too detailed to mention them all here, but after slipping off a chair to the floor at Gaston's feet, A. J.'s body moved as if being examined by a physician as he rolled and tossed back and forth experiencing floods of joy and glory. He writes, in part,

Then came a very interesting part of the experience…. In
vision I was carried to Central America and was shown the
awful condition of the people there. A paroxysm of suffering came
over me as I seemed to be in soul-travail for their salvation.
Then I spoke in tongues as the Spirit gave utterance and in the
vision I seemed to be speaking the very same language of the
Indian tribes with whom I was surrounded.

Then after a little rest, I was carried in vision to South
America…. The vision settled on Brazil, and after another
paroxysm of suffering or soul-travail the Spirit spoke again in
another tongue; then after a little relaxation I was carried to

Chili with the same effects and results; then in like manner to Patagonia…. From Patagonia to Africa and on to Jerusalem, and while there, I endured the most intense suffering as if I might have been suffering similar to that of my Savior on Mount Calvary. I never can describe the awful agony that I felt in my body. After every paroxysm of suffering came a tongue. From Jerusalem I was carried to northern Russia, then to France, thence to Japan; and then I seemed to get back to the United States, but soon I was taken away north among the Esquimaux [Inuits]. While there the language of the Spirit spoken through me seemed similar to the bark of a dog. I was carried to a number of other places in a similar manner…. With all I have written it is not yet told; but judging from the countries I visited in the vision I spoke ten different languages…. Since having received this wonderful experience – being baptized with the Holy Ghost as they were baptized on the day of Pentecost – God has revealed Himself and given many special manifestations of His presence and power in my life. Three times since, the same power has enveloped me and lifted me up from the floor similar to the way He lifted me up the day He came in to abide. Three times during special manifestations of His presence, truthful witnesses have seen tongues "like as of fire" resting near and around my head.

I have traveled thousands of miles and told the simple story and related my experience to thousands of people and have seen hundreds baptized with the Holy Ghost; and every one who received Him spake [sic] in tongues as the Spirit gave utterance. [10]

A. J. Tomlinson was obviously a very intense and passionate person, one for whom drama held some attraction as evidenced by his membership as a young man in the Grassy Narrows literary society and his participation in its drama troupe.[11] In his search for deeper experiences and for an acceptable ecclesiology, A. J. would investigate various denominations and independent groups and attend a variety of public meetings, conventions, or conferences. For example, he visited Frank Sanford's Movement in Shiloh, Maine, at least twice and was baptized by both Brother Gleason, an assistant to Sanford, and by Sanford himself.[12] He was also present at G. D. Watson's convention in Elwood, Indiana, during May of 1903.[13] Harold Hunter shows that A. J.'s travels "introduced him to the ministries of Moody, Robinson, Simpson, Watson, Reese, Knapp, Merritt, Taylor, and others."[14] These influences, the several periodicals with which we know Tomlinson was familiar,[15] and his exposure to the radical holiness practices of Quakerism shaped his life, biblical views, Spirit sensitivities, and missionary activities. He became an indefatigable worker. His leadership skills and commanding presence were almost always quickly recognized by others.[16] He was also quick to apply institutionally what he had learned and experienced personally. In 1913, having not yet been selected as General Overseer for life but well established in his leadership, he summarized qualifications for admitting members into the church:

> The applicants for membership are expected to accept the teaching of repentance, water baptism (by immersion), sanctification subsequent to conversion, the baptism with the Holy Ghost or the sanctified life evidenced by the speaking in tongues as the Spirit gives utterance, the Lord's Supper, feet washing, eternal punishment for the wicked and eternal life for the righteous, divine healing, tithing and offerings, and the second pre-millennial coming of the Lord. Applicants must sever their connection with churches and lodges, if not already free from them (emphasis mine).[17]

A. J. Tomlinson noted various tent meetings, local church services, and General Assemblies that he conducted between 1908 and 1921. Here is one of his early annual summaries of the results of his work:

> Held meetings at tent. Closed out tonight after a ten weeks [sic] successful battle. 225 professions and 163 received the baptism of the Holy Ghost; 78 baptized in water; 106 accessions

to the church. Quite a number healed.[18]

In the midst of such intense Holy Ghost fervor, the church grew from its small beginning in 1902 at the home of W. F. Bryant, in Cherokee County, North Carolina, to some 666 churches and 21,076 members in 1922.[19] By then others with as much or more formal education and business acumen as A. J. had been brought into the movement. Sheer size called for better organization. A change to plural leadership was the result of the decisions of several General Assemblies leading up to the introduction of a formal Constitution in 1921. This Constitution was drawn up by the General Overseer and elders in council and presented to the Assembly by the General Overseer both through his address and by him reading it to the Assembly.[20] After the Assembly's quick acceptance and a thanksgiving prayer to God in recognition of the Holy Ghost, A. J. Tomlinson exclaimed, "Behold what God hath wrought."[21]

After a heart-wrenching nine months,[22] he found its implementation troublesome to the churches and to his office and concluded that a grave error was made in departing from Bible government. A. J. decided to seek the reversal of what he saw as an infringement on the right of way of the Holy Ghost and an undue elevation of Assembly rulings and decisions in regards to the place of the Bible in the church. In short, the Constitution had to be rescinded or the Church of God would be compromised. He referred the matter to the Committee on Better Government, which did not agree with him.[23]

One can only imagine the turmoil within A. J.'s breast and the tension in the Assembly. The unfortunate incidents over the next year resulted in a complete break with a majority of the leadership and membership of the church and a restart for A. J. With the few that remained, he reinitiated, reactivated, or continued what for him and others were the original principles of the movement: The Bible as the Word of God – the church's only law book – and the leadership of the Holy Ghost, which he felt was completely missed in the 1921

Assembly. Daniel Preston, in *The Era of A. J. Tomlinson*, wrote of the break:

> *The seventeenth Annual Assembly held at Cleveland, Tennessee, in the year of our Lord nineteen hundred twenty-two, was the last united Assembly presided over by A. J. Tomlinson.*[24]

On August 8, 1923, at a meeting of representatives from several states in Chattanooga, Tennessee, A. J. Tomlinson and his followers made the decision to,

> *repudiate the Constitution and every other action of past Assemblies that caused the departure from the faith and true Biblical principles, and, by God's permission and help, resolve ourselves back into the Church of God under Bible rule and government.*[25]

This meeting, along with several subsequent actions, led to the convening of a General Assembly on November 22–27, 1923, to affirm and effect these decisions. A. J.'s high regard for the direct and deliberate leadership of the Holy Ghost in the affairs of the church, and his concern that the church defer to and depend upon the Holy Ghost, is seen in his plea addressed to the Holy Ghost during his address to those remaining loyal to him:

> *O, Thou heavenly Dove, Thou hast been thrust aside and grieved –but we have been grieved too. Wilt Thou accept the place in our midst as instructor, guide and ruler according to all the divine plan of our Father God? We want Thee to have due honor, and, if Thou wilt only quicken us to service, we here and now renew our pledge of faithfulness to Thee. We want Thy presence; we want Thy wisdom to be displayed among us; we want Thy power to be demonstrated. We do not want our faith to become attached to human wisdom, but we want it anchored to the power of God – Thou the blessed Holy Ghost. O Thy sacred presence is here. How our souls are delighted with Thee. Please*

never leave us again. If others do not want Thee, we want Thee
to always know that Thou art welcome here. We want Thee to
feel free to move about amongst us as Thou seest best for our good
and the glory of Jesus, whom Thou camest to exalt and glorify.
O heavenly, heavenly Dove, we want to speak good to Thee, we
want to speak good of Thee always. We want Thee to direct this
campaign that is to go down in history as a last days Church
revolution. We know it will go right if Thou hast control. We
will not be deceived by spies who may come into our midst. We
will not be deceived by traitors who may be among us, for we
depend upon Thee. O, Thou Holy One from on high, preserve
and keep us for we are not able to keep ourselves without Thee.
We will continue to look to Thee; we depend upon Thee at all
times. [26]

Not only did A. J.'s 1908 Pentecostal experience influence his
own life, his family's,[27] and the whole Church of God institution
he led through 1922, it was also a major factor in his continuance of
the branch that ultimately became known as the Church of God of
Prophecy by a Chancery Court decision in 1952.[28] A. J.'s plea to the
Holy Ghost (above) in his capacity as leader of the church grounded
the work firmly on the twin principles of (a)the Bible as the Word
of God, and, (b)the Holy Spirit as Interpreter of the Word and the
Teacher, Guide, and Director of the Church. Today both Church
of God of Prophecy and Church of God leadership have shown
sensitivity to the leading of the Holy Spirit in bringing wonderful
reconciliation, fellowship, and cooperation through joint ventures
between these two groups once led in unity by A. J. Tomlinson.
Both movements continue to draw nurture from their deep roots in
Pentecost as witnessed here.[29]

CHURCH OF GOD OF PROPHECY

General Overseers:

Ambrose J. Tomlinson
(1903-1943)

Milton A. Tomlinson
(1943-1990)

Billy D. Murray
(1990-2000)

Fred S. Fisher, Sr.
(2000-2006)

Randall E. Howard
(2006 to present)

Author:

Adrian L. Varlack, Sr.
Church Historian

CHAPTER 9

Elim
Fellowship

FOUNDER:

Ivan Q. Spencer

IVAN Q. SPENCER:
Commissioned for Revival

By Edie Mourey

Ivan Quay Spencer was born November 28, 1888, to homesteaders in the Allegheny foothills of northern Pennsylvania. The second son of Merritt and Alice Spencer seemed destined to farm the family's 160 acres. But stories of early days of Methodism told to the small congregation in the West Franklin Methodist Church gripped young Ivan with a desperate hunger to know and experience God for himself. As he later said, "The calling of God is not necessarily to be a minister or a missionary, but the call of God for you is unto God Himself."

In response to that call, Ivan left the farm in 1909 to attend Wyoming Seminary in Pennsylvania. His leaving, however, was not the result of any encouragement given him by his father.

"What a stupid idea!" his father had bellowed when Ivan told him his intention. "Everyone knows you're a farmer – and a good one, too. Surely the Almighty wouldn't make such a mistake. If you must go to school to prove you're unsuited, go. But not one cent of my money will pay for it!"

That had ended their discussion. But Ivan's pastor suggested he could pay for his books and room and board by selling books to other students at seminary. With his means of self-support secured, he boarded the train in obedience to the call.

Sadly, after just one semester he had to return home. He was very ill with typhoid fever and the school was concerned about him causing an outbreak. Dispirited and sick on the train ride home, he heard God say, "Don't be discouraged, son. I will heal you if you'll trust Me." Ivan affirmed His trust in God, went to sleep, and awoke well. From that moment on, he believed in divine healing, preached it, and saw evidence of it in his ministry.

With this faith-inspiring experience, Ivan did not return to the farm defeated. He was sure of the call and knew somehow, someway, God would prepare him for ministry. In the meantime, he began to tell others of his healing and its availability to them, too. No one in his church or community believed him. The pastor who commended him to seminary said, upon hearing Ivan's testimony, "If I were you … I'd not talk about this to others. You might be misunderstood and be called a fanatic. This could hurt your ministry later on."

Ivan's pastor wasn't the only one who could have tempered the young man's zeal to preach the message of divine healing. His very own mother didn't seem to believe him. This was a great disappointment to him at the time, but he was undeterred.

Life on the farm went on as usual until the day Ivan and his brother, Vern, were forced to go live with their Uncle Elwin Spencer in Elmira, New York. Apparently, a farmer noticed Vern and Ivan coming out of the woods and accused them of hunting out of season. Ivan's father had no choice but to make them move so as to avoid paying any impending fines.

Having both been put to work at a machine shop in Elmira, it became increasingly apparent to Uncle Elwin, however, that Ivan was dissatisfied with his employment. He thought the young man missed being on the farm and working in the soil. He understood that and sympathetically talked to him about the possibility of his finding him employment on a farm somewhere. Ivan was thankful, but told Uncle Elwin, "Of course I'd only want to go for a short while. I've got to preach, you know. But this machine shop just isn't getting me any closer to preaching, and I was farming when God spoke to me before. I just feel like maybe that's where I should be until the way opens up for preaching."

Not soon after, Uncle Elwin secured Ivan work on a farm in Macedon, New York. It was there the young man would hear about Rochester Bible Training School (RBTS) in Rochester, New York, the place that would equip him for ministry.

Marion Meloon described this occasion in *Ivan Spencer: Willow in the Wind – A Spiritual Pilgrimage.* According to her, the farming family and its new hire had finished eating when Ivan began to share his testimony. The farmer's wife seemed to relate to Ivan's experience. She interrupted him at one point to tell of how she had been healed after suffering a serious illness.

"How did it happen? Did God speak to you? Have you told others? What did they think? Do you know anyone else who believes this way?" Ivan couldn't stop asking her questions. She was the first person not only to believe his story, but also to have experienced the healing power of God herself!

It was her answer to the last question – "Do you know anyone else who believes this way?" – that revealed the place where she had been prayed for and received her healing, Elim Tabernacle of Rochester, New York.

Ivan shared his call to preach. The farmer advised, "I'd say if you're called to preach, you shouldn't be trying to farm. Isn't there a seminary you can attend where you can get your training? How about the Genesee Wesleyan Seminary in Lima, only about 15 miles from here?"

"There's a Bible training school connected with the Elim Tabernacle," interrupted the farmer's wife, "that trains ministers and missionaries. It's small, and only a two-year course, but perhaps that is where you should go. Why don't you come to church with us Sunday and see about it?"

The wife's interjection won out. Ivan's curiosity and enthusiasm had been piqued. He had to visit Elim Tabernacle and did so the following Sunday.

Ivan Q. Spencer found his spiritual home at Elim. It was there he first heard divine healing preached and demonstrated again and again. But that wasn't the only "new thing" he saw and heard. He began to witness the wind of the Spirit moving among the people in the church meetings. And so, in the fall of 1911, Ivan enrolled at RBTS, the school associated with the Elim Tabernacle.

The Rochester Elim work was comprised of several ministries in those days. They had opened the Elim Faith Home and the Elim Mission in the late 1890s. At the turn of the century, they began Elim Publishing House, where they printed the *Trust* monthly journal for those of like Pentecostal faith. And, of course, there was RBTS and the church, Elim Tabernacle.

This "powerhouse of the east," as it became known, was an important center of early Pentecostalism. There several early leaders of the Pentecostal movement received their training. Its populace had received the Pentecostal outpouring of the Holy Spirit in the summer of 1907 – just on the heels of Azusa Street.

Upon his enrollment, Ivan had yet to receive the precious baptism, though he had heard it spoken of often. Nonetheless, on one occasion the words of Elizabeth Sisson, famed Bible teacher and Elim guest speaker, convicted his heart. Exhorting her listeners, she said, "To those seeking the baptism, our attitude is now, not of waiting and praying and seeking God, but rather that of 'receiving'; as He breathes out, we can breathe in, and thus may be filled."

Ivan and many others responded to her words at the altar that night. Desperation set in his soul, and from deep within came forth faith for the baptism of the Holy Ghost and fire. He received his personal Pentecost there at the altar – praising God, speaking in a heavenly language, and laughing in the Spirit. His was a full immersion.

Ivan not only received the baptism of the Holy Spirit while at RBTS in 1912, he also received a vision that would chart his future course and rekindle a passion he had felt at the Methodist church of his childhood.

In the vision, Ivan saw Spirit-filled people scattered throughout the world. The purpose for "this world-wide diffusion" as he called it, was for these to "intercede for greater things for the peoples of their respective localities."

X Furthermore, he saw this movement grow in number, but not in power, resulting in a time of sifting and testing that ultimately led to a glorious outpouring. He said he literally saw large, flaming red letters spelling, "REVIVAL." In that moment, he knew he had been commissioned to revival ministry.

Ivan wouldn't have to complete his mission alone. Minnie Back, a young English woman who had become a faithful face at Elim Tabernacle, soon stole his gaze. The two fell in love and were married in 1913. They began ministry together, conducting evangelistic meetings as Ivan continued to farm for their livelihood. Throughout the ensuing years, they evangelized, pastored, and farmed in New York communities like Elmira, Hornell, Reading Center, and Endicott.

In December 1924, while traveling through a blinding snowstorm in order to keep an appointment near Endicott, the Lord spoke to Ivan about opening a Bible school. He heard the Lord instruct him to start a school that trained young men and women for the supernatural ministry of the last hour.

RBTS had continued after the death of its predominant leader, Mrs. E.V. Baker, in 1915. But in 1924 her sisters, who had continued carrying on the work, closed the school. With RBTS closed and this new direction, Elim Bible Institute was birthed in the summer of X 1924 at Endwell, New York. As graduates left Elim and pursued national and international missions, a missionary and ministerial society was formed in 1932 to commission and credential them. Elim Fellowship, as it is known today, thus was born.

These were only the beginnings of Ivan Spencer – short clips of the entire movie of his life. Perhaps men and women like him are best remembered for their passion, the "one thing" they desired. And that for this man was revival.

The passion inflaming his life, ministry, and work had been ignited back at West Franklin Methodist Church. There his pastor preached on the second chapter of Acts. There Ivan, his attention and heart wrapped in awe and wonder at the pastor's verbal portrait, dared to believe, even as a boy, the vivid pictures of tongue-like fire appearing over those gathered together in the Upper Room. There his hopes for a future experience were deflated as the same man who had so moved him said, "Of course, such things do not happen today. The early Church needed signs and wonders to prove the reality of Christ and the Holy Spirit, and to get the Church underway."

But it was too late. Something happened that day to a young boy. Though disheartened, the word pictures had produced something called faith. And that faith, as Ivan would later teach and preach, was a Person; it was Jesus Christ Himself!

Besides, the pastor continued the sermon, and his very next words undermined his own assertion that "such things do not happen today." As he spoke about the early days of Methodism and a certain circuit-riding preacher who held meetings where people acted like those portrayed in Acts on the Day of Pentecost, Ivan began to see the possibility of these things happening in his day.

And that was it. The flame was lit in this youth and set afire in his young adulthood. The large, flaming red letters of REVIVAL consumed his vision, his message, and his life.

Ivan learned that revival made an impact on the Body of Christ personally and corporately. He once said, "Every fresh revival makes Jesus more real, the shedding of His blood more precious and the victories of the Cross more outstanding." So he continued to preach the crucified life, the victorious overcoming life, and the revived life – all made possible only through the cross of Jesus Christ.

One of the added blessings of revival that Ivan sought was the unity of the fellowship of believers. His desire during times of visitation and outpouring was for the Body to be one. An editorial he wrote for *The Elim Pentecostal Herald* was titled, "Unity Paramount." And he believed it. As he asserted, "On the Day of Pentecost, we find men of clashing nationalities, ingrained prejudices and diverse temperaments brought together in a deep heart unity, not a unity in externals, but a unity of heart and mind."

He yearned for the day that brothers and sisters in Christ would come into the unity of the faith.

🖋 So it was only natural that he participated in various moves of God in the earth and that he fellowshipped with other believers in associations and conferences. Ivan attended the constitutional convention of the National Association of Evangelicals (NAE) in May of 1943. He also served on the Board of Administration for the Pentecostal Fellowship of North America from its inception in 1948. He continued to look to the horizon for the flaming revival he saw that day in 1912 and was faithful to prepare the ensuing generations for it until his death on August 17, 1970.

Today, Elim Fellowship continues to thrive as a Christ-centered worldwide fellowship. It is a fruitful branch of the Church universal, cherishing brotherly and sisterly love toward all followers of Christ everywhere and, in addition, seeks to strengthen the Church to reach the world.

ELIM FELLOWSHIP

Presidents:

Ivan Q. Spencer
(1932-1953)

Carlton Spencer
(1954-1985)

Elmer Frink
(1985-1988)

Dayton Reynolds
(1989-1996)

Bernard Evans
(1996-2005)

Ronald Burgio
(2005 to present)

Author:

Edie Mourey
Editor, Furrow Press

CHAPTER 10

Full Gospel Fellowship
of Churches *and* Ministers, International

FELLOWSHIP

FOUNDER:

Gordon Lindsay

GORDON LINDSAY:
God's Barnabas of the Twentieth Century

By Sharon Stover

G ordon Lindsay started a Full Gospel Ministers Fellowship Luncheon in Dallas, Texas, in 1952, to facilitate fellowship and unity among the many Full Gospel churches in the area. His heart was always to unite and bring into close fellowship those of like faith to empower the moving of the Holy Spirit in revival in these areas.

In 1962 Gordon Lindsay became the catalyst for the formation of The Full Gospel Fellowship of Churches and Ministers, International (The Fellowship or FGFCMI). In a letter written to Rev. G. Jerry Bacher, Gordon stated, "We must keep the Spirit of Christ manifested in all of our business to show our brethren that we love, trust, and solicit their fellowship, that this is not a fellowship of cliques, but a fellowship of fellowships."

On September 18, 1962, Gordon Lindsay and a group of 27 other ministers came together for a series of founding meetings at the Baker Hotel in Dallas, Texas. Many of these brethren, who came from formal denominational backgrounds, were a vital part of the *Voice of Healing* magazine. The purpose of The Fellowship was to emphasize, encourage, and promote apostolic ministry, provide ways by which these objectives may be obtained, and provide governmental coverage for ministers, churches, and organizations.

In a December 1962 announcement made in the *Voice of Healing*, Brother Lindsay stated "that all churches which believe in apostolic ministry, regardless of organization, should have a closer fellowship, that there should be a fellowship based on the recognition of the Body of Christ regardless of denominational status.... Many men of God believe that there should be some kind of fellowship that will recognize the fact that all God's people are members of one Body. Such a fellowship would not be another denomination; all churches, as far as it was concerned, would be completely sovereign. These churches or groups of churches would continue their ministry the same as before, but The Fellowship would provide a means by which they could have fellowship with one another, as members of the same body. The Fellowship would not have any ecclesiastical authority whatsoever, but it would assist churches in performing services which they cannot easily or conveniently provide for themselves."

"The life and ministry of Gordon Lindsay, who has been referred to as 'God's Barnabas of the twentieth century,' stands as a beacon to the fellowship, love, and unity of the Body of Jesus Christ. Just as Barnabas of the New Testament recognized the anointing on Saul of Tarsus for the ministry of apostle and evangelist, so Gordon Lindsay, led by the Spirit, recognized the men of our century upon whom the anointing of God rested. Every great ministry in the twentieth century Pentecostal movement and the Charismatic renewal since the 1940s has felt the influence of the life and ministry of Gordon Lindsay.... Gordon Lindsay viewed no man or credible ministry too small to encourage or support."[1]

Gordon was born June 18, 1906, in Zion, Illinois, a Christian dream city founded by John Alexander Dowie, about 40 miles north of Chicago on Lake Michigan. As if fulfilling John Dowie's dream and the city's purpose, Gordon grew up to influence many men whom God greatly used in the healing ministry. Many became world renowned teachers and evangelists.

Gordon's family left Zion and moved to California and then to Huber, Oregon, a small community ten miles west of Portland. Although he was further educated in public schools, Gordon's mother taught him to read. An avid reader, Gordon supplemented his general knowledge by reading hundreds of books, a habit he continued throughout his life. Although unable to attend college because he needed to share the responsibility of caring for his family, he took various correspondence courses, believing nothing is gained by ignorance. This led him to establish various avenues of Scriptural training for ministers on the field and those preparing to go.

Gordon felt the distinct call of God at an early age, but he resisted that call as he grew older. Though reared in a godly home, the community in which he lived did not take religion seriously. Approaching the call from a purely intellectual point of view, Gordon studied Calvinism, observed the futility of death, and remained bored by what he saw in the churches in his community. Nonetheless, his imagination was stirred by the great stories of the Bible and he was thrilled when he read about the life of Jesus. The disconnect between experience and biblical history left him wondering if God had lost His power. Yet he searched for modern miracles as proof that Jesus Christ was the Son of God. Seeing need all around him, he had no answers – only his mother's prayers.

At her invitation this inquisitive young man attended a series of meetings held in a Portland church pastored by Dr. John G. Lake. The noted Rev. Charles F. Parham, who conducted the historic Apostolic Bible School in Topeka, Kansas, was speaking. God touched Gordon and he accepted Jesus Christ as both Lord and Savior. After making a full repentance and restitution for something of which the Spirit had convicted him, he received the baptism of the Holy Spirit a week or so later and spoke in tongues, with a wonderful baptism that forever changed his life and destiny.

Having felt the call to preach the gospel upon his conversion, Brother Lindsay began to travel with Dr. Lake as he held healing campaigns throughout the West Coast. On those campaigns, Gordon experienced the apostolic ministry with signs and wonders following. He realized that miracles were real, seeing them happen before his own eyes, and began praying for a ministry that would reach the multitudes. Knowing he needed to prepare himself for God's answer,

Gordon read everything he could on the subject of apostolic ministry and prayed fervently, waiting on God to send a visitation of His mighty power. He attended two remarkable evangelistic campaigns held in Portland. One was the Billy Sunday meetings, where thousands of people were converted. Charles S. Price conducted the other meetings. Charles Price, however, was forced to terminate his campaign because of violent opposition stirred up against him in the denominational circles. That incident taught Gordon just how powerfully destructive ecclesiasticism could be in obstructing the preaching of the gospel.

Still experiencing the intensity of the call, Brother Lindsay felt God wanted him to begin active ministry. God provided two young men who would travel and work with him: Leon Hall, who became his brother-in-law, and Tom Welch, who had been converted shortly before Brother Lindsay and had a powerful testimony. The trio went to California to see Dr. Lake in hopes he would help them get started. Making the trip to San Diego in an old dilapidated Chevrolet, they connected with Dr. Lake, who offered his tent for meetings and encouraged them on their way. Dr. Lake greatly influenced Gordon during this time, praying him through a severe physical sickness where Gordon learned two great lessons. He stated,

> One was that faith is an act. After prayer is made for healing there is a time to act upon the Word of God. Deliverance came to me at the moment that I acted on the Word of God. Secondly, though it is wonderful to be healed, it is better to be delivered from sickness before it overtakes us. The Word of God teaches that Divine health rather than divine healing is God's plan for the believer.[2]

As Gordon traveled on the evangelistic field, he demonstrated an unusual ability to learn from both the bad and the good. He learned God was able to keep him safe and rescue him from danger. He sadly observed disunity within and between the various Full Gospel churches and their inability to work together. This would later help frame his unifying, encouraging ministry.

In recounting many evangelistic campaigns, Gordon specifically recalled a meeting in Portland, Oregon, during a visit to his home, that yielded only one convert. This lone convert, a young lady, became his wife several years later, on November 14, 1937. In his life story, Gordon said, "Freda was to become a great asset to my ministry."[3] She worked with him in both planting and pastoring churches and holding evangelistic campaigns.

All through the years, Brother Lindsay expected God to do something special, something spectacular that would reach multitudes. He was looking for a restoration of the apostolic ministry that would be greater than ever before. In March of 1947, he received a letter from his good friend Jack Moore, an invitation to come to Sacramento to see the ministry of William M. Branham. William, a Baptist minister who had received the Holy Spirit, had great success in praying for the sick and ministering in Words of Knowledge, with a reported accuracy rate of 100 percent.

Gordon began using his associations within some of the larger Full Gospel circles to arrange some campaigns for Brother Branham, marking the beginning of the organization of great campaigns on an inter-evangelical basis. Until this time, few united Full Gospel campaigns had been undertaken because of doctrinal differences and issues that had caused groups to be suspicious of each other. As a preventive measure, it was deemed necessary that those concerned would agree not to precipitate debate on controversial subjects, but would join together in a united effort to bring the message of deliverance to all the people.[4]

The first meeting, in Vancouver, British Columbia, lasted four days and was an outstanding success. One of the local ministers described it: "Right from the beginning of negotiations for the coming of Brother Branham to Vancouver, a salutary spirit of unity and cooperation prevailed among the Vancouver ministers. This gracious spirit continued, and in fact increased throughout the meetings, and is yet very much a reality finding expression in fellowship groups and meetings."[5]

This newfound unity and cooperation released a great anointing in the meetings. Soon believers from all the various groups were attending. In 1948, the Fellowship saw the need for a publication that would both advertise upcoming meetings and publish the great testimonies of healing and deliverance occurring during the meetings. Since the campaigns were organized on an inter-evangelical basis, the publication would need to be established on this same basis. The *Voice of Healing* magazine was launched, with Gordon Lindsay as the editor. Its purpose was not to argue over doctrine that might precipitate division and confusion among God's people, but rather to proclaim the message of the Great Commission, to minister healing to God's people, and to prepare them for Christ's coming."[6] The magazine began carrying reports of many evangelists and came to represent the deliverance ministry as a whole.

As Brother Lindsay wrote, "When the *Voice of Healing* began its publication, one of the immediate aims was to publicize the full gospel message attractively, and on as large a scale as possible."

The *Voice of Healing* was sent without cost to missionaries and gospel workers all over the world. Sending the magazine to these missionaries brought the news of the deliverance message to key persons on the mission fields. Upon reading the magazine, missionaries in many cases were stirred and began praying God would send a deliverance revival to their field. The *Voice of Healing* headquarters was moved to Dallas, Texas, in 1952. In 1954, the publisher also began publishing books and booklets. Literally millions of faith books have been published since that time. The magazine's name was changed to *Christ For The Nations* in April of 1967.

That Brother Lindsay was called a "Barnabas" is easily understood. He encouraged and served with others to both facilitate large campaigns and enable their ministries, even as he fulfilled the call of God upon his own life.

A pivotal event happened in 1956. Evangelist Jack Coe, who was holding healing meetings across the South, was arrested and jailed in Florida after being accused of practicing medicine without a license. The arrest came after the local Council of Churches banded together and called him a "quack." The Churches of Christ also took the stand that all claims of divine healing were false, and called Coe a "religious racketeer."

Staff from the *Voice of Healing* responded to the accusations with a call to arms and soon the trial gained national attention. Over twenty ministers and evangelists from out of town were sworn in during the historic trial. Standing behind the evangelist, the pastors of local Full Gospel churches stood behind the defense. People prayed and fasted for a successful outcome of a trial that could have affected the freedom to preach the gospel of salvation and healing for years thereafter. Gordon Lindsay personally testified at the trial. The judge eventually threw the case out of court on the contention that Jack Coe had been only praying for the sick according to the tenants of his faith. This was a great victory for apostolic religion in America.[7] The power of a group of ministers and believers banded together, standing for one another and the gospel, was made nationally evident.

In May 1964 the World Correspondence Course was established to help those whose circumstances made it impossible to attend Bible school. This God-given mandate to provide educational opportunities is fulfilling itself even into the next century through the Christ For The Nations Institute founded by Gordon Lindsay in 1970. His wife, Freda, the very person he lovingly called the "great asset to my ministry," would perpetuate the Institute into the following century. Gordon Lindsay passed from this life in 1973, shortly after he and Freda returned to Dallas from a tour of the Holy Land and time spent with family in Spain. The day after their return Gordon preached his last sermon. The following Sunday, April 1, he was called home to be with the Lord during the early part of the Sunday afternoon service at the new Institute building, just before he was to have preached. His last moments were among God's people singing His praises, a fitting end to a life well spent for God. It has been said that you cannot judge a man's ministry until he has died. Looking back, Gordon Lindsay was not only a twentieth century Barnabas, he was a man of vision, anointed by God as a spark that set revival fires spreading from the healing campaigns of the 1940s and into the twenty-first century.

THE FELLOWSHIP
(Full Gospel Fellowship of Churches and Ministers International, Inc.)

Presidents:

John L. Mears
(1962–1963; 1966–1967)

Alfred C. Valdez
(1963–1966; 1968–1970)

Gordon Lindsay
(1967–1968; 1970–1973)

Ralph Hart
(1973–1974)

Russell J. Meade
(1974–1975)

Gene Scott
(1975–1984)

James Helton
(1984–1990)

Don Arnold
(1990–2007)

Gene Evans
(2008 to present)

Author:

Sharon Stover

CHAPTER 11

Independent Assemblies
of God International
(Canada)

FOUNDER:

A.W. Rasmussen

SPREADING THE MESSAGE OF PENTECOST:
A.W. Rasmussen

By Paul McPhail, General Secretary

The Independent Assemblies of God was organized in 1918 by A. W. Rasmussen as the Scandinavian Assemblies of God in the United States of America. Its roots go back to a revival in 1890 among Scandinavian Baptist and Pietist communities. In 1935 at a convention in Minneapolis, Minnesota, they merged with another group named the Independent Pentecostal Churches and adopted the current name, The Independent Assemblies of God International.

Andrew W. Rasmussen was born in Pennock, Minnesota, in 1905, and decided to follow Christ during a revival meeting conducted by evangelist A. B. Ost. He received the baptism in the Holy Spirit during a prayer meeting in Michigan in 1929, the same year the stock market crashed.

In the 1940s a group of people from North Battleford, Saskatchewan, traveled to the William Branham crusade in Vancouver and witnessed the powerful anointing on William's life. The group returned to North Battleford to pray for revival. From that prayer meeting a move of God began in 1948, spreading across Canada. The move of God touched many lives and souls were saved. In fact the Latter Rain Movement in Canada began with the North Battleford, Saskatchewan, move of God. Many ministers left mainline Pentecostal denominations to follow the deeper things of God, the gifts of the Spirit with manifestations and the healing and prophetic gifts. This revival brought new members to the Independent Assemblies of God International (Canada) as ministers sought spiritual and governmental coverings for their ministries as independent congregations.

The Independent Assemblies of God International spread the Pentecost message across Canada and introduced it to other regions like the Eastern Arctic. Rev. John Spillenaer, missionary to the Arctic, traveled by single engine aircraft to isolated Inuit communities. This mission is ongoing to this day with great effectiveness.

The uniqueness of the Independent Assemblies of God International (Canada) is its conviction of the sovereignty of the local church. They believe it is imperative that ministers and churches are able to follow through on the mandate, governed by God without interference from an ecclesiastical hierarchy.

God has raised the Independent Assemblies of God International (Canada) to be an apostolic ministry, with churches and ministries through America, Africa, Canada, Guatemala, India, Mexico, Nagaland, Philippines, Romania, the Canadian Arctic, Northwest Territories, and Argentina. They are, by God's grace, obedient to being an integral part of the continued outpouring of the Holy Spirit, helping fulfill the Great Commission. They are establishing local churches worldwide, supporting missions and missionaries, founding Bible schools and training institutes, and providing accredited correspondence courses.

INDEPENDENT ASSEMBLIES OF GOD INT'L. (CANADA)

First Canadian General Secretary:

Rev. Stanley M. Hammond
(1959-1964)

General Secretaries :

Rev. Harry Nunn, Sr.
(1964-1985)

Rev. Harry Wuerch
(1985-2005)

Rev. Paul McPhail
(2005 to present)

Author:

Rev Paul McPhail
General Secretary

CHAPTER 12

International Church
of the Foursquare Gospel

FOUNDER:

Aimee Semple McPherson

SPREADING THE
FOURSQUARE GOSPEL:
Aimee Semple McPherson

By Jack Hayford

A cross from Los Angeles's Echo Park, where lake fountains send sparkling jets of water nearly 40 feet into the sunlight, sits a church noted for its evangelistic passion, innovative outreaches, works of social compassion, and dynamic, city-impacting ministry, just as it was almost 90 years ago. Multiplied thousands attend every weekend. Transforming ministry flows to hosts of the lost, broken, sick, and needy every day – a tribute, of course, to the present congregation and its leadership. But it also serves as a commentary on the durability of the spiritual dynamic that laid the foundation for Angelus Temple in 1923 and the eventual birth of the International Church of the Foursquare Gospel.

What began at one church, Angelus Temple, in the early twentieth century has extended into the twenty-first, to a constituency of more than eight million believers in 142 countries, where continued outreach and growth is occurring through more than 60,000 congregations. The founder of this global Pentecostal fellowship is Aimee Semple McPherson, whose ministry began as a missionary in China when she was 20 years old. It concluded at her death 34 years later in Oakland, home to California's largest public arena, where she was conducting a citywide evangelistic campaign.

Aimee Elizabeth Kennedy was born October 9, 1890, near Ingersoll, Ontario, Canada, the only child of James and Minnie Kennedy. Although reared in a Christian home, Aimee would later recount how she began to question Bible truths during her teen years. While still a 17-year-old high school student, Aimee attended a revival service conducted by Pentecostal evangelist Robert Semple. Intending to mock those in her village called "holy rollers," Aimee found her heart pierced by the evangelist's call to repentance and new birth. Resistant at first to the message, the presence of the Holy Spirit penetratingly spoke to her heart, convicting her of her sin, prideful unbelief, and need for a Savior. In her biography she described struggling with conviction for three full days until, finally surrendering to God, she knelt in prayer, lifted her hands to the Lord and asked Jesus to be her Lord and Savior. The clarity of her experience emphasized the reality of Christ to her. Having asked Him to forgive her, she felt the burden of sin roll away and the glory of the Lord fill her heart. She had been born again. There on her knees, alone in God's presence, she began to sing the hymn "Take My Life and Let It Be." From that day those words became the governing sentiment of her life (McPherson, 1923, 39).

Within days, as she attended the evangelistic meetings and heard Robert Semple speak on the baptism with the Holy Spirit, Aimee began to be consumed with the desire to experience this "Pentecostal baptism." After earnestly seeking God in prayer, she was "gloriously filled with the Holy Spirit." She states, "Jesus was more real and near than the things of earth round about me. The desire to praise and worship and adore Him flamed up within my soul" (McPherson, 1923, 45). With that desire, one that would never leave her and one that fed her passion to spread the gospel, came a love and compassion for souls and a longing to serve the Lord that would stay with her throughout her lifetime. All who worked closely with Aimee were consistently amazed by her zeal for the work of the Lord and her unrelenting commitment as a genuine "laborer in the harvest" – a zeal and intensity of pursuit many attribute as one of the factors that weakened her resistance in later years and likely contributed to her physical vulnerability and early death at age 54.

The revival meeting that so dramatically changed her life spiritually also changed her life romantically. As Aimee continued to attend the extended series of revival services, she became personally acquainted with the evangelist, nine years her senior. The handsome Robert Semple won Aimee's heart, and though he traveled to another city to conduct evangelistic meetings, he returned to discuss marriage with her. During that season, God had filled Aimee with a call to ministry. Thus, their joint desire to serve the Lord contributed to their sense of His having fit them together perfectly. Robert and Aimee Semple were married in August 1908, and almost immediately began the process of preparing to go as missionaries to China.

In 1910, shortly before Aimee turned 20 years old, she and her husband of less than two years set sail for China, where they had committed to serve and spread the gospel. It seemed to the young couple that they would enjoy a lifetime together, preaching the Word of God and ministering to those for whom the Lord had so burdened their hearts. But that was not to be. Robert Semple died in Hong Kong three months after their arrival, and Aimee was left penniless and alone, waiting for the imminent birth of her first child. When her daughter, Roberta Star Semple, was a month old, Aimee returned to the United States, facing life as a single mother.

Back in the United States, Aimee Semple began to make the necessary adjustments to provide for herself and Roberta. Within two years of her return, she met and married a businessman, Harold McPherson, a committed believer who acknowledged God's touch on his wife's life and assured her of his support if she were ever to return to ministry. But Aimee hoped to be able to settle down to a "normal" home life. As the probing of God's Spirit continually pressed her call to Christian service and ministry, she began to wrestle with the inescapable clarity of that call in contrast to her preference to be a housewife and godly church member.

Knowing she was not being obedient to her call began to wear on the young mother, and her physical health declined. She had two major surgeries within a two-year period, and she continued to grow weaker and weaker with each passing day. During that time, God continually knocked at the door of her heart asking, "Now will you go?" (McPherson, 1923, 78). Convinced that it was either "go" into the ministry or "go" through an untimely physical death, Aimee answered "yes" to God's call. As she yielded, almost immediately she was healed. From that day, she never questioned her call and her assignment to preach the gospel.

Vowing to keep her solemn promise to the Lord in spite of her feelings of inadequacy, Aimee Semple McPherson began evangelizing and holding tent revivals. Starting on the East Coast of the United States, she soon expanded to other parts of the country, meeting with surprising success. People gathered in ever-increasing numbers to hear the remarkable lady evangelist. When she was not meeting in a tent, she arranged for the largest auditorium in whatever city she was in so she could accommodate the record number of people who attended. Decades later, other Pentecostal denominations acknowledged Aimee's pivotal influence in the birth of many of their churches in the Eastern and Midwestern United States.

Since cities and towns of that era (1916 through the early 1920s) often had only one venue that could accommodate crowds of substantial size, "Sister," as she asked she simply be addressed, had to share the time with whatever competing "event" was being held in town. On one occasion she had to hold her meetings in a boxing ring before and after a boxing match. Once in San Diego, the National Guard had to be brought in to control the crowd of more than 30,000. People often stood in line and waited for several hours to be assured of seats for the next service. Sister McPherson preached a positive message that exalted Jesus and showed the face of a loving God. Her frequently outstretched arms invited people to a full-hearted, Spirit-filled commitment to Christ, describing a life of dedication and service to Him as being the only life that offered true fulfillment.

Instead of having rigid expectations for people who attended her meetings, Aimee welcomed everyone. God was no respecter of persons, and neither was she. She preached a gospel of repentance and believed strongly that everyone in the world had the right to hear the gospel. Sister McPherson preached to the social elite of the day, but also reached out to the poor and the disenfranchised members of society. She evangelized in the South at a time when segregation was rampant. Although she invited all to attend her meetings, she often went to the "black" parts of town and held meetings following her main meetings. Aimee broke down racial barriers everywhere she ministered. She even had great success spreading the gospel to a gypsy community after the chief's wife and the chief himself were healed in a Denver revival meeting. Sister McPherson is also credited with helping many of the Hispanic ministries in Los Angeles get started. With Aimee Semple McPherson there was no color, ethnic, or status separation line. Her love for and acceptance of people from every walk of life endeared her to untold numbers of people. From her humble start as an itinerant evangelist, Sister McPherson eventually held meetings all over the world.

Weary of traveling constantly and having no place to raise a family, Aimee sensed God directing her to move with her children to Los Angeles in 1918. This was after Harold had expressed his inability to fulfill his earlier pledge to partner with her in ministry. They separated amicably, and Los Angeles became her base of ministry operations as she continued citywide crusades. During those years of continual travel, she began to raise money for the building of Angelus Temple. It was dedicated on January 1, 1923 – a stunning structure for its time, a timeless facility that still effectively hosts large crowds. When Sister McPherson was only 32 years old, God graced her with ministry that filled the near 6,000-seat auditorium three times each Sunday and often at regular weekday meetings. Hundreds came to Christ every week; miracles of healing abounded. In response to the desperate need of families in the Great Depression, Angelus Temple provided a commissary and community services that were more reliable than the city's own relief programs. As growth continued, LIFE Bible College was born and became a ministry-training center. Churches were planted across the United States, and missionaries were commissioned as she called for those who would go "around the world with the Foursquare Gospel."

The name of the movement derived from a sermon Sister McPherson preached in Oakland, California, in 1922 – a message based on Ezekiel's vision. The following is taken from that sermon, which was printed in its entirety in *The Bridal Call* in January 1923:

> *And I looked, and, behold, a whirlwind came out of the north, a great cloud, and a fire infolding itself, and a brightness was about it, and out of the midst thereof as the color of amber, out of the midst of the fire. Also out of the midst thereof came the likeness of four living creatures. And this was their appearance; they had the likeness of a man. And as for the likeness at their faces, they four had the face of a man, and the face of a lion, on the right side: and they four had the face of an ox on the left side; they four also had the face of an eagle.*
>
> *"And from out the midst thereof – out of the midst of the cloud of Grace – there comes the four-square Gospel of our Lord and Saviour Jesus Christ, as four living creatures, having the likeness of a Man. What a glorious gospel it is, with straight feet sparkling like burnished brass, and with rushing, mighty, tender feathered wings that turn not as they go but bear "straight forward" the glory and the majesty of the great Jehovah Jirah! As these were "living creatures" so is the gospel living, moving, vitally alive. The Gospel which is borne to us is indeed a four-square Gospel, facing the world four-square, revealing four different faces or phases of the Gospel, all of which bear faithful likeness to the man Jesus Christ" (Ezekiel 1:4, 5, 10, KJV).*
>
> • *The face of the man: Jesus Christ, the only Savior*

- *The face of the lion: Jesus Christ, the baptizer with the Holy Ghost*
- *The face of the ox: Jesus Christ, the great physician*
- *The face of the eagle: Jesus Christ, the coming king*

As the Temple became the spiritual home for thousands and the Bible college grew, churches were planted throughout the greater southern California area. Graduates of the college soon scattered across the nation, taking with them the full gospel message. Some went in response to requests that the Foursquare movement begin churches in their communities; others returned to their home towns to begin Foursquare churches. It was this growth that soon evolved into a church organization.

Sister McPherson was always looking for creative ways to present the gospel. While holding a revival meeting in San Francisco in April 1922, Sister McPherson became the first woman to preach a sermon over the radio. Intrigued with the possibilities that medium seemed to offer, she purchased a radio station herself, and The Foursquare Church maintained that station, KFSG, until 2003. Through her use of the medium of radio, Sister McPherson soon had one of the most recognizable voices in the world – not just in the church world. Every city where services were held usually had in attendance civic leaders as well as pastors representing the local churches of every denomination. She made sure that Angelus Temple was represented in local parades and entered floats in the famous Rose Parade in Pasadena. Her illustrated sermons attracted even those from the entertainment industry, looking to see a "show" that rivaled what Hollywood had to offer. These famous stage productions drew people who would never have thought to enter a church; then those people who had gone to see the "show" were presented with the message of salvation. Aimee believed that the gospel was to be presented at every opportunity to as many people as possible. She used all the means at her disposal to do just that.

Sister McPherson once wrote, "You don't need to be an orator.

What God wants is plain people with the Good News in their hearts who are willing to go and tell it to others. The love of winning souls for Jesus Christ sets a fire burning in one's bones. Soul winning is the most important thing in the world. All I have is on the altar for the Lord, and while I have my life and strength, I will put my whole being into the carrying out of this Great Commission" (qtd. on Foursquare website, www.foursquare.org).

"Sister," as Aimee Semple McPherson was affectionately called by the thousands to whom she ministered, went to be with the Lord, September 27, 1944, while conducting a revival service in Oakland, California. A memorial service was held on her birthday, October 9, at Angelus Temple. Upon her death, her son, Rolf K. McPherson, became president of The Foursquare Church. He served in that position for 44 years, providing stability, strength, and growth to the fledgling denomination that his mother left behind.

International Church of the Foursquare Gospel

Presidents:

Aimee Semple
McPherson *(1927–1944)*

Rolf K. McPherson
(1944–1988)

John R. Holland
(1988–1997)

Harold E. Helms
(1997–1998, Interim)

Jared D. Roth
(2004, Interim)

Paul C. Risser
(1998–2004)

Author:

Jack W. Hayford
(2004–2009)

Glenn C. Burris, Jr.
(2009 to present)

Jack Hayford

CHAPTER 13

International Pentecostal Church *of* Christ

FOUNDERS:

Paul T. Barth
(IPA)

John Stroup
(PCC)

BEARING THE COST OF PENTECOST:
John Stroup

By Clyde M. Hughes

Born on a farm on a fall day in 1853, not much about John Stroup's origin would foretell the changed lives which would follow in his shadow. Little is known about either his youth or early faith. But after the Ohioan married, he found himself regretful about beating a horse. Going home, he asked his wife, Sarah, to pray with him. Feeling unsuccessful at that effort, he learned a church had placed their names on their membership roll. After awhile, a church representative came to collect money for the pastor. John quickly told the would-be assessor that if the preacher would work like he did, help from others would not be needed. That ended his connection with churches for awhile. But after a time of seeking God in his home, the barn, and the woods, John gave his heart to the Lord at the age of 24.

Soon afterwards, a minister friend invited him to a meeting. On the way to church he asked John to preach, and Stroup consented. For his first sermon he used John 3:7 as a text: "Ye must be born again." The new Christian made a few halting statements, but mainly gave his personal testimony of how he had been washed by the blood of Jesus. He would later write that it was a short sermon, if it could be called a sermon at all. After the message, he turned the service back to his friend for its conclusion. The whole experience made him feel very insecure about his ability to preach, but he felt much better after family prayer that night.

Not many days hence, he received another appointment to preach at a schoolhouse about four miles from his home. A large crowd had gathered and heard him preach from Matthew 7. Perceiving another poor job of preaching and not wanting to face any of the people, he hastened ahead of them to his horse and rode into the woods. Tying up his mount to a sapling along the path, he knelt to pray. There he tarried with his Father until he was soothed by the Spirit of God.

Coming from a Wesleyan background where a belief in the "second blessing" was prevalent, John believed it to be for him. In August of 1878 he visited a camp meeting in Urbana, Ohio, where he stood to say, "I've come here to this campground to get sanctified!"

The leader of the meetings asked, "How much do you want it? Enough to go to this altar?"

John replied, "Yes sir!"

He claimed the experience came to him around five or six in the morning and that it was accompanied by "a falling out under the mighty power of God." From then on, he was a strong advocate for the experience. Many claimed to have been sanctified through his preaching, which also brought him ridicule of his new and extreme views. His ardent seeking of sanctification would be typical of the earnestness of a life to come, in which he always sought more of God. As a staunch holiness preacher, a hallmark of his preaching was a second definite work of sanctification, which was then understood to be the baptism of the Holy Ghost.

Serving as a conference evangelist for the Wesleyan Methodist Church in western Ohio, he attended a camp meeting at Dunkirk, Ohio, in 1907. It was there John first heard about the Pentecostal blessing. He would write:

There were three of us who were holding a camp meeting. One evening one of the brothers and I walked out on the campgrounds and the brother sat down on a stump. While there, the third brother came up and the one with me began talking to him about some converts in his church and the other brother, whose name was Morgan, told him that a sister in his church had received the baptism of the Holy Ghost and "spoke in tongues." The brother on the stump was very much opposed to it. After listening to them for awhile I said that most of us have tongues enough. The camp meeting ended. I went home. I never thought much more about "tongues" until later that fall.

I made up my mind I would try to find out about this tongue movement, as most people called it. Before I started to Kenton, I went upstairs to my room, took my concordance and began to look up the word "tongue," and put every place down on paper where the concordance said anything about tongues in the Bible.... The next morning I arose real early to look up the references on tongues from the building of the tower of Babel found in Genesis 11:6–7, to the last words Paul had to say about tongues in 1 Corinthians 14:39 when he said, "forbid not to speak with tongues." I at once saw it was dangerous to silence people who were speaking with other tongues; and for the first time in my life I found out I never did have the baptism of the Holy Ghost and fire as at Pentecost in Acts 2:4. I made up my mind I would let the people alone that spoke in other tongues. I began to tell my wife and children that none of us had the baptism of the Holy Ghost as they got it at Pentecost because none of us had spoken in tongues....

The next morning I was up early reading my Bible about Pentecost and was so interested that I missed the morning train I had intended to go home on. I had to take a trolley car and go another way in order to get home that day. So I went to the trolley car station and got me a ticket to Mt. Cory, Ohio, in order to get a car home that day. On entering the car I sat down by a young brother I knew, and at once we entered into a conversation.

He said, "Brother Stroup, what do you think about the baptism of the Holy Ghost and speaking in tongues?"

"Well," I said, "it is in the Bible. But I don't know whether the people in Findlay had it or not."

At once he said, "I have got the experience."

If the bottom of the car had fallen out I would not have been more surprised than hearing him say that he had the experience. This brother and I only rode together about twelve miles, but it was the shortest twelve miles that I ever took. I had known the young man for some time and he was always so quiet, never having much to say. I believed every word he said about it and about speaking in tongues. I told myself he surely has something I never saw him have before for now he loves to talk about the Holy Ghost."

God used this man and two other people to influence John toward seeking the baptism. John Stroup wrote that he sought for the baptism of the Holy Spirit a total of six weeks in 1908. During this period, he decided to seek God all night long. About this time, he felt the Lord had told him to get rid of his farm, worth $25,000 in those days, and be left with just his Bible as his possessions. He said he turned it all over to his family. His remaining possessions amounted to just over eight dollars. He said he gave it all to God, "down to a ten penny nail." Reading that Jesus said, "The foxes have holes and birds of the air have nests, but the Son of Man hath not where to lay His head," he became so broken up for the love Jesus had for him that he was overcome with weeping.

When John accepted that there was a third experience called the baptism of the Holy Ghost and that at its reception a person would speak in tongues as the initial evidence, his family took strong exception. Two of his sons came to him to inquire about his wanting to speak in tongues, trying to dissuade him. Sarah said the boys were about out of their minds trying to change John's mind, but to no avail. John said he intended to have the baptism of the Holy Ghost if everybody in the country lost their minds. It is said that Sarah had once found him in the home seeking for the baptism of the Holy Ghost and shoved him onto the floor in her antagonism to the proposition of Pentecost. Later, in his booklet, *What God Can Do*, he rejoiced that she, too, became convinced of the Pentecostal way and received the baptism in 1910.

He received a letter from the president of his denomination saying, "Brother Stroup, I am sorry you have gone off into this movement that our conference does not endorse which has brought so much confusion into our churches. So I do not care to any further endorse you as our conference evangelist, and would be glad if you would resign as such." John states that it cost him something to be true to God and to his convictions. His credentials expired on August 27, 1908, so he looked into the Radical United Brethren group. The credentials committee examined him, but when they asked him if he would preach and teach that speaking in tongues was the evidence of receiving the baptism of the Holy Spirit, he said that was his position. His application was rejected.

To have a place to preach the Pentecostal message, he purchased a tavern in Findlay, Ohio, and converted it into a mission. The upper story was used to house a school for teaching others about the baptism. John was preaching a revival in town at the Methodist church in the evening and attending morning services at T. K. Leonard's Workers Training School, which had a mission. So John was both preaching and seeking.

On a Tuesday, at 10:00 a.m. September 22, 1908, just after leading the chapel service, John stood and said, "I know there is nothing between God and me."

A brother told him, "If there is nothing between God and you then raise your hands and reach for God!"

John said he raised his hands and put everything he had into reaching for God. The power of God fell on him, knocking him to the floor. While there, he had a seven-fold vision. He was being tied to a stake to be burned, and the Holy Spirit asked him if he would be willing to be burned at the stake for the sake of Jesus and the gospel. Next he was arrested by three policemen and taken to jail. "Would he be willing to die in jail?" Then he was at sea in a ship that was sinking. "Would he be willing to die in the sea?" After that, he was taken to the penitentiary and locked in a cell. "Would he be willing to die there?" Again he was onboard another ship with blue colors. He was asked if he would be willing to be drowned in the depths of the sea. He was taken to an insane asylum. "Would he be willing to die there?" Lastly, he was in a railroad wreck. His back was on the rail and the wheels of the train just inches away, ready to cut him in two. Once again he was asked, "Would he be willing to die for the sake of the Lord and the gospel?"

Each time he resounded with a, "Yes!" To John Stroup, the baptism of the Holy Ghost was not a badge to wear, but a resource for a costly and deeper walk with a holy God. He later reported that all this had occurred as fast as his thoughts could go. At that point he saw the Holy Ghost coming and covering him. He was baptized in the Holy Ghost and began to speak in tongues.

After founding the Pentecostal Church of Christ, the organization he loved, in 1917, he served as its General Overseer for twelve years. He is believed to be the first to take the Pentecostal truth to both southern Ohio and eastern Kentucky. In 1929, upon his receiving the ultimate baptism, his self-written obituary was read:

And on September 22, 1908, about 10:00 a.m., he received the baptism of the Holy Ghost in an upper room in Findlay, [Ohio], while leading the early chapel service, as the 120 did on the Day of Pentecost (Acts 2:4, 'And they were all filled with the Holy Ghost and began to speak in tongues as the Spirit gave them utterance'). And on the 10th day of May, 1917, he organized what is known among us as Conference Number 1 of the Pentecostal Church of Christ at Advance, [Kentucky]. This closes the life's pilgrimage of our brother. He has had seasons of great rejoicing in closing up his life's journey in his last illness.

International Pentecostal Church of Christ

Pre-International Pentecostal Assemblies:

Philip G. Wittich
(1919-1936)
President, National & International Pentecostal Missionary Union

Paul T. Barth
(1921-1939)
Founder; Chairman, Association of Pentecostal Assemblies

International Pentecostal Assemblies
Chairmen:

John W. Pitcher
(1936-1938)

Ernest F. Ruff
(1938-1941)

Roy S. Dunbar
(1941-1951)

James A. Keiller
(1951-1962)

William M. Spencer
(1962-1970)

General Superintendent:

Thomas G. Grinder
(1970-1976)

Pentecostal Church of Christ

Bishops:

John Stroup
(1917-1929)

Martin A. Hay
(1929-1938)

General Overseers:

E. Lindsey Cyrus
(1938-1954)

Chester I. Miller
(1954-1976)

International Pentecostal Church of Christ
General Overseers:

Chester I. Miller
(1976-1982)

Thomas G. Grinder
(1982-1990)

General Overseer, Bishop, and Author:

Clyde M. Hughes
(1990 to present)

CHAPTER 14

International Pentecostal Holiness Church

FOUNDERS:

Ambrose Blackmon Crumpler

Gaston Barnabas Cashwell

INTERNATIONAL PENTECOSTAL HOLINESS CHURCH:
Roots and Spiritual DNA

By Doug Beacham

Through several streams of gospel witnesses, International Pentecostal Holiness Church (IPHC) Ministries traces its theological roots to the Book of Acts. These streams directly include the Azusa Street revival of 1906, the eighteenth and nineteenth centuries Wesleyan Holiness Movements, and the sixteenth century Protestant and English Reformations. Indirectly, the streams include the faithful witnesses to the gospel found in the other main component of Western Christianity, the Roman Catholic tradition. These roots are reflected in our affirmation of the Apostles' Creed, the Nicene Creed, and antecedents from the Thirty-nine Articles and Augsburg Confession reflected in our Articles of Faith.

The direct spiritual DNA of IPHC Ministries began in the late nineteenth century as two holiness streams, originally independent of each other, were brought together by regional proximity, relationships among leaders, and particularly the impact of the Azusa Pentecostal experience. The two streams originally represented divergent parts of the United States, with the Fire-Baptized Holiness Church (FBHC) originating in the Midwest, and the Pentecostal Holiness Church of North Carolina (PHCNC) originating in eastern North Carolina.

IPHC origins are traced through the lives of four men. B. H. Irwin founded the FBHC. Through him Joseph Hillery King of Georgia entered the story. Ambrose Blackmon Crumpler founded the PHCNC and it was through that gate that Gaston Barnabas Cashwell entered. Gaston Cashwell became the catalytic figure who contributed to these holiness churches accepting the Azusa Street Pentecostal experience and ultimately uniting in 1911 to form the Pentecostal Holiness Church.

B.H. Irwin, J.H. King, and the Fire-Baptized Holiness Church

Originally born and reared in Missouri, B.H. Irwin moved to Nebraska, where he studied and practiced law until his conversion in the late 1870s. His ministry was originally in Baptist churches, but in the late 1880s and early 1890s he was exposed to the growing Holiness Movement. The first national holiness camp meeting west of the Mississippi River was held in 1873 in Cedar Rapids, Iowa. The movement grew in the West. It was through the Iowa Holiness Association that Irwin began to shift in his theology and church relationships.

By 1891 Irwin claimed he was sanctified and his theology took on elements of John Wesley and particularly John Fletcher. Fletcher had described the "baptism of burning love." Sometimes he termed it the "baptism with the Holy Ghost and with fire," which he believed followed the second blessing of Wesleyan sanctification. Through Fletcher, Irwin developed his distinctive contribution to Pentecostal history and theology of the baptism with the Holy Ghost and fire.

Irwin began to preach this in Wesleyan Methodist and Brethren in Christ congregations in the Midwest. He claimed that he personally received this baptism while in Enid, Oklahoma, in October 1895. Nonetheless Irwin's theological shift from classic holiness theology, along with the highly charged emotional elements of his services, led to a break with the Iowa Holiness Association. In response to the rejection of his message and style, in late 1895 Irwin formed his own "Fire-Baptized Holiness Association."

By 1896 he was ministering in southern states among

Wesleyan Methodist congregations. Over the next two years he began to form Fire-Baptized Holiness Associations in Florida, South Carolina, North Carolina, Tennessee, and Georgia. His young organization grew quickly and associations were established in Kansas, Oklahoma, Texas, and even in Canada.

A significant event occurred in 1898 when Irwin returned to northeast Georgia to minister in the town of Royston, the home of the soon-to-be famous baseball player Ty Cobb. A young Georgia Methodist preacher named Joseph Hillery King (1869-1946) attended the services. Joseph King was committed to the holiness wing of Methodism, a position many Methodist leaders and congregations were beginning to abandon.

In late July and early August the same year, Irwin took the bold step of calling the various state associations together to form a national organization. This "General Council" met in Anderson, South Carolina, where a fully developed theological statement and government were presented and adopted. Besides the various state leaders, Joseph King was also present for the meeting. He had left the Methodist Church to join Irwin's Fire-Baptized Holiness Church.

Of particular note to Pentecostalism were these three statements in its Constitution:

> We believe also that the baptism of the Holy Ghost is obtainable by a definite act of appropriating faith on the part of the fully cleansed believer.

> We believe also that the baptism with fire is a definite, scriptural experience, obtainable by faith on the part of the Spirit-filled believer.

> We do not believe that the baptism with fire is an experience independent of, or disassociated from, the Holy Ghost. . . .

It is important to remember that this "baptism with the Holy Ghost and fire" was not about speaking in other tongues. The standard Wesleyan and post-Wesleyan holiness view was that sanctification and the baptism with the Holy Ghost were the same experience; the terms were considered interchangeable. Irwin claimed a spiritual experience beyond justification and sanctification, an experience rooted in "fire," and in a greater dimension of Holy Ghost experience.

Irwin's significance is that over eight years prior to Azusa Street and a couple of years prior to Charles F. Parham's Topeka, Kansas, "Pentecost," the theological concept of a third blessing distinctly related to the Holy Spirit had been introduced into the Holiness Movement. It is likely Parham heard Irwin preach of this third blessing and provided some of the theological construct for what occurred in Topeka at the turn of the century.

In late 1899, Irwin began publishing *Live Coals of Fire*. Joseph King later wrote that "it was the first paper in the United States that taught that the baptism of the Holy Ghost and fire was subsequent to sanctification." The young Joseph, then thirty, had moved to Toronto, Canada, to pastor and was the ruling elder of the FBHC in Ontario. Nevertheless in 1900 Joseph was thrust into the leadership of the young organization when Irwin confessed to moral failure. The fledgling FBHC began to fragment with the loss of the charismatic founder. Nonetheless, Joseph King was able to sustain the church in Georgia and the Carolinas, bring some theological order to some of Irwin's more extravagant claims, and provide an organizational structure that balanced Irwin's autocratic model.

Irwin's post-FBHC life is sketchy. Final reports of his life and ministry reveal he lived in northern California, attended the Azusa Street revival, and apparently had some level of local ministry in the remaining years of his life.

A.B. Crumpler and the Pentecostal Holiness Church of North Carolina

Under the leadership of Ambrose Crumpler (1863-1952), the Pentecostal Holiness Church (also known for a time as the

Holiness Church) originated in eastern North Carolina. Ambrose was from Clinton, North Carolina, and as a Methodist evangelist had success in the 1890s in preaching Wesleyan holiness. His fiery preaching drew large crowds, and his emphasis on sinless perfection drew the ire of the Methodist Church. By November 4, 1898, his controversy with the Methodist Church had reached such a point that he and a small group of like-minded Methodists formed a congregation in Goldsboro which they named "The Pentecostal Holiness Church."

By late 1899 charges were brought against Ambrose in the Methodist Church for continuing to hold services without the permission of local Methodist ministers. Though acquitted of violating church law, Ambrose was finally convinced he could not continue to serve within the Methodist structure. By early 1900 he formed a new movement using the same name as the local Goldsboro congregation. In 1901 he began a paper, *The Holiness Advocate*, which lasted for seven years.

The theology of the new group was centered around justification by faith, sanctification as an instantaneous second work of grace, divine healing as provided in the atonement, and the premillennial second coming of Jesus Christ. As with most of the Holiness Movement, sanctification and the baptism with the Holy Spirit were considered the same spiritual reality.

At the same time that Ambrose's movement was being organized, a layman named Julius Culbreth established the Falcon Camp Meeting in the little village of Falcon, North Carolina, in July 1900. This camp meeting became a significant southern networking venue for holiness preachers and leaders from across the United States and Canada. Relationships grew between King's Fire-Baptized Holiness Church and Ambrose's Pentecostal Holiness Church through this camp meeting (which continues today). (The movement dropped the name "Pentecostal" prior to Azusa Street but added it again after the West Coast revival.)

As the young PHCNC developed from 1901 through 1906, it

faced a series of potentially fatal disputes over divorce, remarriage, tobacco, and the financial crisis of the original Goldsboro congregation. As word of the Azusa Street revival began to spread in the summer and fall of 1906, many ministers in Ambrose's movement were weary of conflict and longed for spiritual revival.

G.B. Cashwell and the Azusa Street Revival

Gaston Cashwell (1862-1916) was another eastern North Carolina minister who had a profound impact on most of the Holiness Movements in the southeastern United States. Though his early years were turbulent, Gaston came to Christ around 1897, was sanctified soon afterwards, and joined Ambrose's Pentecostal Holiness Church in 1903. From 1903 through 1906 the middle-aged Gaston preached in various Pentecostal Holiness congregations and farmed to provide a livelihood for his family.

Like many in the small movement, Gaston was frustrated with the church's struggles. As he read of the continuing Azusa Street revival in Los Angeles, his heart burned to personally encounter this new experience. Following prayer with his wife, the couple sacrificed to purchase Gaston a one-way ticket for a six-day train ride from North Carolina to Los Angeles.

Upon arriving in California in mid-November, Gaston Cashwell, like many others, was overwhelmed, and somewhat put off, at the racial diversity and other aspects of the services. As a southerner growing up in reconstruction and the emergence of Jim Crow laws, there was a cultural bias related to the African American leadership of the revival.

Gaston wrote, "I had to die to many things, but God gave me the victory. I struggled from Sunday 'til Thursday . . . [before going forward] in earnest for my Pentecost." It was not only the racial issue that presented a hurdle for Gaston; he also faced a new theological paradigm.

William Seymour's Azusa theology had adopted a three-fold sequence of grace-filled operations: justification by faith, sanctification, and the baptism with the Holy Spirit as a third experience separate from sanctification. Following Parham, Seymour had also connected speaking in other tongues as the initial evidence of the third experience. Both elements were new theological aspects that Gaston recognized as sources of potential conflict in the Pentecostal Holiness Church of North Carolina.

Gaston remained in Los Angeles for several weeks before returning in December. During this time he preached in the Los Angeles area, wrote an article for Seymour's *Apostolic Faith* magazine, and was presented a new suit and return ticket to North Carolina.

Upon returning to Dunn, Gaston began plans for a special service on New Year's Eve, 1906. He invited people in his own movement and the Free Will Baptist Church. Renting a tobacco prize house near the railroad in Dunn, many gathered to hear his story. A.B. Crumpler had already scheduled special services in Florida and was not able to attend; however, he did not hold Gaston in high regard and began to inform people that he would oppose him if he preached the Azusa doctrine.

Gaston's service did not disappoint. On December 31 spiritually hungry people received their Pentecost and spoke in other tongues. Several were healed. Word quickly spread that people were speaking in tongues. What has been termed "Azusa East" began. For the next three weeks hundreds came to Dunn from across North and South Carolina, Virginia, and Georgia. By the end of the services, key leaders from the PHCNC, the Free-Will Baptist, the Fire-Baptized Holiness Church, and some African-Americans, had received their Pentecost.

By the latter part of January, Gaston was traveling to various churches with the Pentecostal message. In February 1907 he was in Toccoa, Georgia, where Joseph King was leading a local FBHC congregation. Members of the church had gone to Dunn, received their Pentecost, and invited Gaston to preach. At first Joseph was opposed to the message. Though he accepted a third blessing called the "baptism with fire and the Holy Ghost," he did not accept that speaking in other tongues was the initial evidence. As the Toccoa revival continued, however, the Holy Spirit led him to a renewed study of Acts and he came to the conclusion that Gaston was correct. Joseph received his Pentecost experience and led his entire movement into accepting the new theology.

A few months later Gaston was instrumental in influencing N.J. Holmes of Greenville, South Carolina, and M.M. Pinson in Birmingham, Alabama, as they received their Pentecost. With Presbyterian roots, Holmes led his Altamont Bible School (now Holmes College of the Bible) into the experience, and Pinson later became one of the founders of the Assemblies of God. Gaston traveled extensively throughout 1907 in almost all the southern states and into Oklahoma. He met Charles Mason in Memphis while on these journeys. In October 1907, Gaston took the significant step of beginning his own magazine in Atlanta, *The Bridegroom's Messenger*. For the next three years, it was the primary mouthpiece of southern Pentecostalism.

In early 1908 Gaston traveled to Cleveland, Tennessee, for the annual meeting of the Church of God. A.J. Tomlinson received his Pentecost, thus leading his movement into the Pentecostal camp.

But things were not going well back in Ambrose Crumpler's church. Along with a small group, Ambrose, though having spoken in tongues, rejected the theological argument of the rising Pentecostal movement. The crisis came to a head at the November 1908 annual conference. Though reelected unanimously as leader, Ambrose Crumpler walked out of his own movement when the delegates affirmed a change to the theology which adopted the Azusa construct.

In 1909 Gaston's influence in the movement began to wane and by 1910 he was no longer the leading figure. By the November 1910 meeting of the PHCNC, Gaston was dropped as a member. While there is some mystery surrounding this event and his later years, there is no doubt that Gaston Cashwell was the single most instrumental person the Holy Spirit used to bring and promote the Pentecostal message in the southern United States between 1907 and 1910.

The International Pentecostal Holiness Church Today

Gaston's influence was a factor as King's Fire-Baptized Holiness Church and the Pentecostal Holiness Church of North Carolina began serious discussions of a merger in 1910. The two groups formally merged in Falcon, North Carolina, on January 31, 1911. Through this consolidation, which adopted the FBHC theology model and the PHCNC name, the movement was able to gain strength and grow into the twenty-first century.

INTERNATIONAL PENTECOSTAL HOLINESS CHURCH

*Bishops:

Samuel D. Page
(1911–1913)

George F. Taylor
(1913–1917)

Joseph H. King
(1917–1946)

Daniel T. Muse
(1937–1950)

Joseph A. Synan
(1945–1969)

Hubert T. Spence
(1945–1946)

Paul F. Beacham
(1946–1949)

Thomas A. Melton
(1946–1953)

Oscar Moore
(1953–1957)

Julius F. Williams
(1969–1981)

Leon O. Stewart
(1981–1989)

Bernard E. Underwood
(1989–1997)

James D. Leggett
(1997–2009)

Ronald W. Carpenter
(2009 to present)

Author:

Doug Beacham

*More than one bishop served at one time until 1969.

CHAPTER 15

Open Bible Churches

FOUNDERS:

Fred Hornshuh, Sr.

John R. Richey

FRED HORNSHUH, SR. AND JOHN R. RICHEY:
Fiery Evangelists

By Wayne Warner

Robert Bryant Mitchell, in commenting on his *Heritage & Horizons: The History of Open Bible Standard Churches*, wrote, "The very heart of this history is the story of men and women of God who were ardent seed sowers, evangelists, builders, pastors, and teachers."

Two of the more prominent of that group, Fred Hornshuh, Sr. and John R. Richey, experienced amazing triumphs of faith that beg to be retold for this twenty-first century. For that reason we look at the pioneering exploits of these two men who founded the Pentecostal groups that merged to create the Open Bible Standard Churches, now Open Bible Churches.

Fred Hornshuh, Sr. (1884-1982)

If you were to inquire about a legendary preacher in the U.S. Northwest by the name of Fred Hornshuh, Sr., you would get a variety of answers. The first person might tell you that Fred was an aggressive, early Pentecostal evangelist associated with Florence Crawford, the Azusa Street Revival veteran and founder of Portland Apostolic Faith. The next person might tell you they remember him as the founder of the Bible Standard Mission, a forerunner of the Open Bible Standard Churches.

Many would say Fred Hornshuh, Sr., who passed gospel torches to his son Fred, Jr. and many others when he died in 1982 at the ripe old age of 98, was bigger than life.

Fred was born on a cold winter day in 1884 in a small community near Oregon City to a mother who was 50 years old. She and her godly husband, nineteenth century German emigrants, had prayed for a son who would enter the ministry. In preparation for that calling, Fred's early education included a one-room school, two years at John Alexander Dowie's Zion College in Illinois, and Willamette University in Salem, Oregon.

As a child Fred knew he would become a minister, but by the time he graduated from college he had drifted from his childhood experience. Following the death of his father in 1908, Fred agreed one evening to attend a cottage prayer meeting with his mother. That meeting would change his life and set him on a near non-stop ministry for the Kingdom.

"I had such an exceptional conversion," he testified later, "that I jumped to my feet and praised God audibly." His reaction stirred the other 25 people at the meeting, and they praised God with him. The enthusiasm still burned in his heart when Fred reached 90, as he told a Portland *Oregonian* reporter: "Years ago when people were converted, everybody knew it."

A year after his conversion, Fred received the baptism in the Holy Spirit and began to minister with the Apostolic Faith. Following his marriage to Beulah Fern Calkins, Fred preached wherever he had opportunity on the West Coast. His skid row ministry reached missions in Portland, Los Angeles, Oakland, Tacoma, Seattle, Vancouver, B.C., and other cities.

When his mother bought them a 40 x 60 foot tent, the couple conducted Pentecostal services throughout western Oregon and Washington. Often Apostolic Faith churches sprang up following their street meetings and old-fashioned revivals.

Fred would forever praise God for bringing Beulah into his life. "She was an exceptional help in music, playing her guitar, singing solos, accompanying the congregation on the organ or piano, and also playing her saxophone."

Sorrow gripped their hearts when they lost their five-year-old daughter, Laverna, to diphtheria. But their lives were joyful when they saw their other children, Lorena, Fred, Jr., and Waletta, dedicate their lives to the Lord's service.

One of the tent meetings proved to be a long-standing connection in Eugene, Oregon, beginning in 1914. Pat Hegen and his wife, Mary, who was Fred's sister, accompanied Fred and Beulah to town, where they set up their gospel tent at 11th and Oak. Although the Pentecostal movement was 14 years old at that time, no Pentecostal work had been started in this university city of 10,000. The team, as was their practice, took their musical instruments to street corners and attracted crowds with their singing. Each would give their testimony, and Pat and Fred would take turns preaching to passersby. At the close of the street meeting, the team would encourage listeners to follow them back to the tent for the evening service.

While Pat Hegen assumed leadership of the Eugene group that was meeting in a rented hall, the Hornshuhs packed up their tent and struck out for other needy harvest fields, which included missions in Portland.

Fred's emphasis in the pulpit was on the unsaved. And he usually had sinners repenting at his altars. When criticized for not preaching deeper sermons, he countered with, "How many have you dug out of sin and hell?"

That usually took care of the criticism.

The Apostolic Faith spread its influence throughout the Northwest with the likes of the Hornshuhs; Hegens; Harry R.R. Neat; Earl Crook and his wife (sister of Beulah Hornshuh); Joseph Conlee, whose personal testimony is featured in the tract, *The Lonely Cabin on the Forty Mile*; and other dedicated soul winners leading the way.

Fred Hornshuh appreciated the ministry opportunities with the Apostolic Faith, but disagreed on church polity with Florence Crawford, which resulted in a split in 1919. Fred led a group that called themselves the Bible Standard Mission. Eugene became the headquarters for the new group, and Fred – knowing the power of the printed word – founded *The Bible Standard*, a monthly magazine.

The Eugene church asked Fred to return as pastor, ushering in one of Eugene's finest hours. The church grew and made plans to build a larger complex. The result was the 3,000-seat Lighthouse Temple, second in size for Pentecostal churches on the West Coast to Aimee Semple McPherson's Angelus Temple in Los Angeles. Popular evangelists such as McPherson, Kathryn Kuhlman, Smith Wigglesworth, and Dr. Charles Price filled the temple in the late 1920s.

Radio station KORE's manager saw the excitement around 12th and Olive and offered Hornshuh free air time for the Sunday evening services.

Things were going well at Lighthouse Temple, but Fred Hornshuh was an evangelist and church builder. He resigned in 1930 and moved south some 150 miles to Klamath Falls, Oregon, where he built another church. Other pastorates would follow for Fred. From Klamath Falls he moved to Tacoma, Washington, and built Faith Temple debt free. Then it was across the country to St. Petersburg, Florida; Pontiac, Michigan; and back to Portland.

As one looks at the contribution Fred Hornshuh, Sr., made to the Kingdom, perhaps the greatest was his love for souls and the founding of what is now known as Eugene Bible College. Did he ever retire? At his memorial service a granddaughter, Jan Kent, remembered him for his lifelong commitment: "He never stopped ministering," she told the crowd.

The February 1938 *Open Bible Messenger* published one of his sermons and closed with an appeal that reflects his mission in life: "Let us make a covenant with God and with one another that we will pull sinners out of the fire and snatch them as brands from the burning. Love, faith, and prayer mixed with works, zeal, and pluck will do exploits."

Doing exploits. That pretty well sums up the life of Fred L. Hornshuh, Sr.

John R. Richey (1899-1984)

The second person who fits the bill for R. Bryant Mitchell's "ardent seed sowers, evangelists, builders, pastors, and teachers" was reared as a poor Kentucky farm boy with a fifth grade education who migrated to Los Angeles in 1920. In Southern California John R. Richey found the "pot at the end of the rainbow" when he discovered the Pentecostal experience through Aimee Semple McPherson's International Foursquare Gospel.

John not only was baptized in the Spirit and trained for the ministry, but he also found his life companion, Louise Hansen, a young Iowa woman who had also migrated to Southern California and was enrolled in McPherson's Bible college. Louise's Pentecostal introduction came in Iowa when she was healed of a goiter through the ministry of evangelist Maria Woodworth-Etter. The couple gained valuable experience at Angelus Temple and by pastoring Foursquare churches in the Los Angeles area. John would be the first to say that had it not been for Louise, he would never have been the leader that he became.

In a contact that would later pay eternal dividends, the Richeys made a trip to the Northwest from Southern California in 1927. A stop in Eugene, Oregon, and a visit with Fred and Beulah Hornshuh and their Lighthouse Temple gave the Richeys a look at one of the most successful Pentecostal pastorates outside of Los Angeles. Little could these couples realize this brief contact would be a stepping stone to bring together in 1935 the Bible Standard and the Open Bible Evangelistic Association.

Committing their lives to the Lord and to wherever He would send them, the Richeys were enjoying a thriving ministry in Southern California when a call came from the Midwest in 1928. Louise had earlier felt a call to return to Iowa for ministry, and now the couple found themselves as pastors of two churches in Des Moines, Iowa. In addition, John served as Midwest superintendent for Foursquare.

Despite the Great Depression crashing in on Iowa and the rest of the states, the Pentecostal group in Iowa and Minnesota grew rapidly. Tent meetings that John organized stirred communities and churches were born overnight. "Have faith in God" seemed to be their guiding light when funds were short during these desperate times. John Richey soon built up a large congregation as scores were converted, baptized in the Spirit, and healed. By faith he established a radio ministry that cost $150 a week – a huge sum in those days.

He soon became known as a dynamic leader, with Foursquare graduates following him to the Midwest to evangelize and pioneer churches. New converts eagerly enrolled in the Midwest Prepatory Bible School (later Open Bible College), which John founded in his church, formerly the Grace Methodist at 19th and Crocker in Des Moines, Iowa.

But they faced many challenges.

When vandals set fire to a Des Moines tent and burned it to the ground in the middle of the night, John got on the radio and the phone. By the next night the debris was cleaned up and a new and bigger tent was in its place. Crowds were bigger than ever. Des Moines residents were amazed and exclaimed, "You just can't stop that preacher Richey."

Another crisis hit hard when a lumber supplier threatened to padlock the doors of the soon-to-be dedicated Fort Des Moines church if the lumber bill was not paid immediately. Richey went to prayer and felt led to ask a church member, Carrie Hardie, for $6,000. She withdrew the money she had invested in the Iowa Power and Light Company and lent it to John. Later the Power and Light Company fell on hard times during the Depression and was unable to pay investors, but John paid the money back to Mrs. Hardie with interest and thus preserved her savings.

With prayer, faith, and determination, John Richey and his followers spread throughout Des Moines. At one time they were operating 12 churches in the city.

R. Bryant Mitchell, one of the founders of the Open Bible

Evangelistic Association who would later serve as general chairman, described what he saw in the early days of John Richey's leadership. "Services were held in the old-fashioned revival style of the early days of American evangelism. Creeds, rituals, church forms, and standard denominational methods were abandoned. The common people, many of whom had not been churchgoers, went to join the crowds. The sick were prayed for and healed. Hardened sinners wept for mercy. The people laughed, shouted, clapped their hands, and praised the Lord as they sang…. Seekers spent whole nights in prayer seeking the Holy Spirit's endument of power, and praying for a revival. Great joy filled the hearts and homes of those touched by this revival."

Another secret for success was standing on the Word. While pastoring his church at 19th and Crocker in Des Moines during the 1930s, the Richeys claimed Jeremiah 33:3: "Call unto me, and I will answer thee, and shew thee great and mighty things, which thou knowest not."

A break in relationships with the Foursquare came in 1932 when Richey and 31 other ministers in the Midwest disagreed with Sister Aimee over ownership of local church property and her remarriage after a divorce. They appreciated Sister but they were dividing over principles which they felt were important. After negotiations failed to solve their differences, the Midwest group withdrew peacefully and formed the Open Bible Evangelistic Association. It was a small Depression-born organization but filled with enthusiasm, which inspired church members to witness, pray, and sacrifice to local and foreign missions.

John R. Richey was at the helm during turbulent times, but the ship remained on a steady course. As it turned out, the Open Bible Evangelistic Association became a short-lived church organization because John began to talk with Fred Hornshuh and other leaders of the Bible Standard in the Northwest about a merger of the two groups. Those negotiations brought the merger in 1935 when the Open Bible Standard Churches was founded with 70 churches and

210 ministers.

John and Louise Richey continued in leadership with the new organization, leading the Open Bible Institute, and pastoring First Church of the Open Bible in Des Moines. But after completing 10 years in leadership in 1939, the Richeys felt the Lord leading them into traveling evangelism. In 1944 they found themselves full circle, back in Pasadena, California, where they had pastored before beginning their ministry in the Midwest.

Here they leased the Layne Memorial Tabernacle and started a day and night prayer revival, which lasted for a full year with no days off. "This was during World War II," John later related. "Folks were praying for their sons in the service." The telephone they installed in the prayer room was busy with people calling in requests.

"Prayer was their life," former secretary Ruth Dunlap Douglas wrote. "My apartment was located beneath their bedroom. I would go to sleep hearing them praying and awake to the sound of fervent prayer."

The group later purchased other property and John Richey started the California Open Bible Institute.

After retiring from pastoral ministry, the Richeys went on the road again conducting prayer revivals. Scores coast to coast who attended their meetings could testify of receiving healing and the baptism of the Holy Spirit under their ministry.

Early in their ministry the Richeys learned they would never have children. But God promised they would have spiritual children. They went to their graves in 1984 and 1986 seeing the fulfillment of that promise many times over.

OPEN BIBLE CHURCHES

General Chairmen:

John R. Richey
(1935-1947)

Everett J. Fulton
(1947-1953)

R. Bryant Mitchell
(1953-1967)

General Chairmen:

President:

Ray E. Smith
(1967-1976; 1979-1995)

Frank W. Smith
(1976-1979)

Jeffrey E. Farmer
(1995 to present)

Author:

Wayne Warner

CHAPTER 16

Open Bible Faith Fellowship *of* Canada

FOUNDER:

Armand O. Ramseyer

AT THE RIGHT TIME WITH THE RIGHT TOOLS:
Armand O. Ramseyer

By Melissa Cassidy and Don Bryan

Armand Orrey Ramseyer was born in New Hamburg, Ontario, Canada, on July 28, 1914, the ninth of eleven children. He grew up on a farm and attended a one-room schoolhouse through the eighth grade, at which time the family's financial situation necessitated his going to work.

Age 19 found Armand working at the Merchants Rubber Factor in Kitchener. There he met Hilda Weicker, who also worked at the factory. The couple married December 25, 1934, a Merry Christmas indeed. December, 25, 1935, brought another Merry Christmas, with the birth of Armand, Jr. Three years later a daughter, Janet, entered the scene. It was also the year that Jesus entered the scene for both Armand and Hilda. Shortly after their conversion they were asked to help with street meetings in the surrounding villages, and the Lord saved many people through that ministry.

In September 1940, the Ramseyers were invited to pioneer a ministry in a small village several miles from Kitchener. Armand continued to work at the factory and pastored the small church in Doon, Ontario. There, Paul, son number two was born. At this same time Armand began a radio ministry, The Happy Hour, with a children's choir formed in the Doon church. This ministry blessed many people.

In September 1945, the Ramseyers left the Doon church and began a new work 70 miles from Toronto in Waterloo, twin city of Kitchener, using the local mason hall. The radio broadcasts expanded with the help of the local people who listened and wanted to become part of that ministry. The Ramseyer children, Bud, now eight, Janet, five, and Paul, three, became the youngest trio to sing on radio. Daddy sure was proud! In 1946, son John was born.

Armand was ordained with another Pentecostal organization, but had been dropped due to differences over the gift of prophecy. Armand stated, "I believe the Holy Spirit is able to speak in the English language as well as in other tongues. They do not really uphold the gift of prophecy, which I shall never deny, under God." In 1948 a minister friend invited Armand to attend a convention of the Open Bible Churches in the United States, in Springfield, Ohio. The fellowship at the convention was such that Open Bible invited Armand to become a part of the organization.

Armand's Waterloo congregation began construction on a new building in 1949. Upon completion, the group became proud members of the first and only Open Bible church in all of Canada. To share this joy was the latest addition to the Ramseyer family, Elizabeth, born March 22, 1950. With the building program behind him, Armand began schooling again and received his bachelor and masters degrees in theology. Son Timothy chose this time, October 1, 1952, to complete the family.

In the spring of 1954, Armand was asked to pastor a church in Massachusetts. He approached the Pentecostal Assemblies of God in Canada and arranged to have the assets of the Open Bible Church sold to them. He went ahead to the U.S. and the family stayed behind for a short time to finish school, sell their home, and say goodbyes. Once the immigration papers were completed, the family reunited once again, with the exception of Bud, who remained in Kitchener to continue his employment. During this pastorate Armand earned his doctorate degree in theology. The church grew. In 1958, the family purchased a 32-foot trailer and entered the evangelistic field.

While holding evangelistic meetings in Aberdeen, Washington, the church's pastor asked Armand if we would consider accepting the pastorate there. In November 1959 the Ramseyers accepted and moved their now larger home, a 50-foot trailer, to the land of liquid sunshine. The ministry in Aberdeen was again a building ministry. The church began in an old house which was soon condemned. The small congregation loved and worked hard with the Ramseyer family to erect a new church building.

It was hard for the Ramseyers to say goodbye to Aberdeen, but the Lord made His calling known to Armand in July 1965, when the congregation of Open Bible Chapel in Concord, California, requested him to pastor their church. Again, the Lord blessed the church with growth.

Armand became a spiritual father to many in the area, including a group of young people who also became spiritual fathers to others. Until a series of heart attacks and subsequent open heart surgery in 1972, Armand could be found, it seemed, anywhere and everywhere at the right time – praying for the sick, sitting with the lonely, and rejoicing with those who rejoiced. He was a familiar figure in many family gatherings. He could be found with everything in his hands, from a Bible to a plunger, successfully accomplishing whatever task was needed. His generous nature earned him many friends. His hard work earned him much respect. Graciously the Lord allowed Armand to see many events come to pass He had revealed to him before Armand died of leukemia in his home January 29, 1976.

Since the church in Waterloo had been the only Open Bible work in Canada, Open Bible Canada lay dormant until the '70s, at which time Harry Armoogan, a Trinidadian, felt called to Canada. Harry was born into a devout Hindu family in Golconda Junction, Trinidad, a small, rural, sugar cane community. Along with his three cousins, Noel, Emmanuel, and Keith, Harry came to Christ at an open air meeting conducted by Dhasniha Mahabir in Golconda Junction in the late 1950s. Though all four men suffered persecution, they became part of the St. John's church, which Mahabir established, and remained dedicated to their newly discovered faith. Emmanuel eventually became pastor of the St. John's church after Mahabir stepped down, and Keith became field director of Open Bible Standard Churches of Trinidad and Tobago, following the tenure of Dr. Don Bryan, a missionary who served as field director from 1956-1969.

Harry became an ordained Open Bible minister. He was among a group of nine people (four of them Armoogans) in the second graduating class of Trinidad's Open Bible Institute, class of 1959. Since the Armoogans lived in a remote village, they had to walk through cane fields and down rural roads to get to school, an approximate 45-minute journey, and then trek back home late at night.

All nine graduates became pastors of churches they pioneered. Following is an excerpt from the book *Relay of Faith*, giving more detail about the Open Bible Institute:

> *"Between the years 1958-1961, student teams founded more than fifty percent of the works started in those early days... Student teams were dedicated to the cause of the gospel and equipped with a vision of their own people lost and heading to a Christ-less eternity. Many of them weathered great opposition and hostilities in order to proclaim the gospel to those who would listen. They took their message everywhere throughout the length and breadth of the island."[1]*

Harry pastored the Open Bible Church in Sedras for two years and then Jordan Hill for several years. When he migrated to Montreal, Canada, he did not find an Open Bible Church to attend. After two years, he moved to Waterloo. Again, he found no church link with Open Bible, so he decided to start something for Open Bible himself. He wrote Open Bible's General Superintendent Ray Smith, asking for permission to use the Open Bible name and proceeded to register Open Bible in Canada. As he pursued this course of action, he learned about Alex Ness, who had left the Pentecostal Assemblies of Canada and started a thriving work in

Toronto. Alex had connected with Dr. C. Russell Archer, Open Bible's (U.S.) Eastern Division Superintendent from 1977 through 1998.

Harry learned that Dr. Ness had attempted to register Open Bible in Canada but found it had already been registered by Armand Ramseyer in 1947, although the registration was dormant. Alex Ness reactivated the Open Bible registration and became the first President (later General Superintendent) of the Open Bible Organization in Canada. He brought John Owens, Jr., from the U.S. to serve as Vice President.

Having founded three Toronto churches: Lakeshore Cathedral, Queensway Cathedral, and Metropolitan Evangelical Centre, Alex was experienced and well connected. A missionary statesman, he traveled extensively around the world. He authored several books, including *Triumphant Christian Living, Pattern for Living,* and *Holy Spirit Volumes I and II.* He also worked with Morris Cerullo, who at that time was conducting salvation/healing crusades in the United States and Africa.

Harry Armoogan was elected as the third General Superintendent and served in that position more than five years, establishing a firm footing for Open Bible in Canada. During Harry's term of office, C. Russell Archer visited Canada many times as General Overseer. In 1994, Harry visited Kenya and felt the Holy Spirit tell him that he was to personally reach out to that country. During his next ten years pastoring another Open Bible church in Toronto, Harry traveled to Kenya nearly every year. He would eventually start a mission station there.

In 1993, Dr. Peter Morgan contacted C. Russell, whom he had met 12 years earlier, with the intention of bringing his church in Brampton under the Open Bible banner. Bramalea Christian Fellowship was a thriving, debt-free, multi-cultural church in a suburb northwest of Toronto. Peter wanted a covering and relationship with trusted, mature men of God such as he had seen in C. Russell and Open Bible's Eastern Region.

`After many hours of discussion in his office in Vandalia, Ohio, C. Russell suggested that Peter bring his church under Open Bible in Canada rather than the United States. As C. Russell discussed this with the Canadian Board of Directors, they decided to invite Peter Morgan to be their Canadian General Superintendent. A large new sign was erected in front of Bramalea Christian Fellowship to show their affiliation with Open Bible.

Although a new chapter had now opened for the Open Bible Standard Churches of Canada their growth continued slowly, resulting in only four churches by 1995. In the spring of 1995 Peter Morgan heard about the vision of Peter Youngren, President of World Impact Ministries, to launch churches across Canada and made an appointment to visit with him. With most humble intentions Dr. Morgan offered Open Bible Standard Churches of Canada to Rev. Youngren as a vehicle to advance the gospel in Canada. Peter Youngren had been looking for a registered organization so he could credential ministers working with him.

Within a few short months a new constitution was adopted and the name was changed to Open Bible Faith Fellowship (OBFF) of Canada. The first directors included President Peter Youngren, Vice-President Peter Morgan, Secretary George Woodward, Treasurer Lindsey Burt, and Directors Randy Neilson, Ron Cosby, Dwain Peregrym, and John Burns. These men of God, who pastored influential churches from coast to coast, brought national representation to Open Bible for the first time in its Canadian history.

Open Bible Faith Fellowship was established on a model that allowed for local church autonomy with accountability to the Fellowship. It quickly became apparent this fellowship model would need an Executive Director to see the growth that God had indicated was possible. Rev. Randy Neilson was appointed to this post and invested the next seven years traveling across Canada, visiting pastors and leaders to encourage their participation. This model of ministry made OBFF one of Canada's most rapidly developing church groups. By 2003 it had more than 90 churches and 450 credential-holders across Canada. Although there had been rapid advancement, the time had come to adjust the leadership paradigm.

The fall of 2003 brought a significant shift to the leadership of OBFF with the departure of Rev. Neilson to become an Open Bible pastor in Florida and the resignation of Rev. Peter Youngren. After a one-year term as OBFF President David Youngren and the Board of Directors contacted the well-respected Rev. Rick Ciaramitaro of Windsor, Ontario, and asked if he would consider becoming the Canadian President. Rev. Ciaramitaro, who 23 years earlier had pioneered what had grown into a 2,000 member church (Windsor Christian Fellowship), humbly agreed with the condition that all of the Directors across Canada would become mentors for the pastors in their regions. With this new ministry model OBFF has continued to thrive.

In 2006 Rev. Rick Ciaramitaro and the Board of Directors of the Open Bible Faith Fellowship of Canada were granted affiliation with Open Bible Churches (U.S.A.) and recognition with the Department of International Ministries. In God's timing, Armand's dream had come to pass.

OPEN BIBLE FAITH FELLOWSHIP OF CANADA

Presidents/General Superintendents:

Richard Lewis
(1989-1990)

Alex W. Ness
(1982-1988)

Harry Armoogan
(1990-1995)

Peter Morgan
(1994-1995)

Peter Youngren
(1995-2003)

David Youngren
(2003-2004)

President:

Rick Ciaramitaro
(2004 to present)

Authors:

Melissa Cassidy

Administrator, Open Bible Faith
Fellowship

Don Bryan

Executive Director, Mission USA
Open Bible Churches

CHAPTER 17

The Pentecostal
Assemblies *of* Canada

PAOC APDC

FOUNDERS:

Robert E. McAlister

Andrew H. Argue

A LEGACY OF DISTINCTION:
R.E. McAlister and A.H. Argue

William A. Griffin

Not all Pentecostals are entirely comfortable talking about founders or fathers of their movement which emerged in the early years of the twentieth century. The restoration of the New Testament Church's emphasis on the role of the Holy Spirit and the manifestation of spiritual gifts was a "God thing" for which no one could take credit. The Pentecostal movement was, as Carl Brumback put it, "a child of the Holy Ghost."[1] Charles Parham, often referred to by outside observers as the father of the movement, declared, "There is no man at the head of this movement. God Himself is speaking on the earth."[2] Indeed, the first historian of the Pentecostal movement, Bennett F. Lawrence, expressed the general viewpoint of early Pentecostals: "This movement has no history. It leaps the intervening years, crying 'back to Pentecost.'"[3]

Canadian Pentecostals, whether because of some innate reluctance or perhaps historical uncertainties, do not refer to any person as the founder of The Pentecostal Assemblies of Canada (PAOC). That is not to say there is any shortage of notable men and women of God who played significant roles in proclaiming the Pentecostal message across the nation. While the great Azusa Street revival provided the sparks which ignited full gospel works around the world, a uniquely Canadian form of Pentecostalism emerged in a small mission led by James and Ellen Hebden at 651 Queen Street in Toronto. According to her own testimony, Ellen Hebden was alone in her room seeking God for more power in her ministry when suddenly, in a remarkable way, she sensed the presence of the Holy Spirit. In the midst of her expressions of praise she repeated an unknown word several times.[4] The date was November 17, 1906. The next day Mrs. Hebden announced to people at the mission that she had received the baptism of the Holy Ghost. Within a few months, her husband, James, and about 80 believers had received their baptism and spoken in other tongues.

The importance of the Hebden Mission in the history of Canadian Pentecostals cannot be overemphasized. Within five years from its beginning, there were at least a dozen "latter rain" churches in Ontario that were related in some way to the Hebden Mission. Many missionaries such as the Chawners, Atters, Randalls, and Lawlers were either sent out or encouraged in some fashion by the Mission. The Hebdens developed significant relationships with a veritable "who's who" of early leaders of the movement in Canada – names like G. A. Chambers, A. G. Ward, and R. E. McAlister. Even Aimee Semple (later McPherson) and her husband attended meetings in the Toronto mission before leaving for China. Mrs. Hebden once said that Aimee's "gift of interpretation was such a blessing in giving to us the very words in given tongues that it made the presence of God very manifest to all."[5]

But having noted the prominence of the Hebden Mission during the early years of Pentecost in Canada, it must be reported that the Mission played no role whatsoever in the founding of the PAOC as a chartered religious entity. Indeed, Mrs. Hebden fought tooth and nail against any attempts to organize the movement. In a strongly worded article in the *Promise*, she declared, "Not only is the free leading of the Spirit against man-made organizations, but the unity of that Spirit demands its abolition."[6] Eventually this fierce opposition to organization along with Mrs. Hebden's penchant for directing individuals through prophetic utterances gave way to the apparent need for order and accountability. As historian Thomas Miller observes,

Though services at her mission continued at least until 1914, the moral and legislative leadership had passed to those men who united in 1919 to form The Pentecostal Assemblies of Canada. By this time other workers, such as A. G. Ward, G. A. Chambers, John T. Ball, R. E. Sternall, R. E. McAlister, and A. H. Argue, had emerged as recognized leaders of Pentecostalism in Canada.[7]

In keeping with the purpose of this book to highlight the ministries of founding leaders, Robert E. McAlister and Andrew H. Argue have been selected, somewhat arbitrarily, as representatives of all the men and women who contributed to the beginnings of The Pentecostal Assemblies of Canada (PAOC).[8] Robert McAlister was the dominant figure in Eastern Canada and clearly the most influential person in the administration of the PAOC for more than a decade after its formation in 1919. Andrew Argue was the point person when the Pentecostal work took shape in the city of Winnipeg. He was well known for his evangelistic campaigns throughout Canada and the United States. The family names McAlister and Argue have been prominent for the entire history of the PAOC as relatives and descendants have ministered with distinction.

Robert Edward McAlister

R. E. McAlister (just R. E. to those who knew him well) played a pivotal role in the establishment of early Pentecostalism in Ontario. His life story is one of the outstanding biographies of the Canadian Pentecostal revival. He was born in 1880, near Cobden, Ontario. His Scottish Presbyterian ancestors had been part of the Holiness Movement which was known for its lifestyle of "separation from the world" – and that included the latest fashionable dress. Men, for example, were expected to reject "showy white shirt fronts" and neckties were denounced as prideful and wasteful of the Lord's money. Holiness people were to avoid church entertainments, secret societies, games of chance, and buying life insurance.[9] This stern morality and personal self-denial was an integral part of Robert's upbringing. He experienced a personal conversion at the age of 21. Responding to a call to ministry, he attended God's Bible School, a new holiness college in Cincinnati founded by Martin Wells Knapp in 1900. Although illness forced Robert to leave the school before completing the second year, he became an evangelist in the Holiness Movement Church established by Ralph C. Horner in 1895. His association with this holiness group is significant since Horner had added a "third blessing" (a fire baptism) which could easily be converted to the Pentecostal baptism in the Holy Spirit.

While conducting evangelistic meetings in one of Horner's churches in Western Canada, Robert heard about the outpouring of the Holy Spirit in Los Angeles and decided he had to check it out. He arrived at the Azusa Street Mission on December 11, 1906, received his personal Pentecost, and within a few hours headed for home with a new experience and a new message. His immediate status with the Holiness Movement is not clear, but by 1908 he was clearly on the way to developing an "apostolic faith" church in Ottawa, the nation's capital. He also itinerated throughout Ontario and Western Canada, holding meetings with groups who embraced the baptism in the Holy Spirit accompanied by tongues. In January 1910, after holding meetings in Winnipeg, Robert returned to Toronto to participate in a Pentecostal convention sponsored by the Hebdens. Comments made by Mrs. Hebden in *The Promise* indicate that his ministry was well received:

> *Bro. McAlister from Winnipeg just opened his mouth and out of his inner being flowed rivers indeed of living water till the vessels in the household of God were filled again and again with bread and wine of the kingdom of God. It was just the pure Word of God administered in season to many, accompanied by the Holy Ghost.*[10]

Many years later, PAOC historian Gordon Atter, who had

known Robert very well, declared him to be one of the greatest of the first generation of Pentecostal preachers in Canada. At that time, according to Atter, a preacher who did not move about in a vigorous style on the platform was considered a "dud." Robert, however, rarely moved. He had a rather monotonous type of delivery and tended to preach long sermons. Yet, Atter added, "He was one of the greatest preachers we had because of his material. He never went into the pulpit but what he was completely prepared.... When he was through, you would remember that sermon, and his altar calls were tremendous.[11]

In May 1911, Robert launched his first publishing venture, *The Good Report*, which gave information on upcoming meetings as well as reports and testimonies of healing. One of the most outstanding incidents concerned the healing of Mrs. Charles E. Baker. She had cancer and was facing a second operation when she went to the Apostolic Faith meetings at Robert's church in Ottawa and received a miraculous healing from the Lord. As a result of his wife's healing, Charles Baker gave up his Ottawa business and entered the Pentecostal ministry. He became the first General Treasurer and served with Robert, who became the first General Secretary when the PAOC received its federal charter in May 1919. Robert's most significant contribution in the publishing field was the creation of *The Pentecostal Testimony* in 1920, still the official publication of the PAOC. The *Testimony* was an important unifying agent for the thin band of Pentecostal groups that stretched from coast to coast.

Though lacking advanced formal education, Robert was a pastor, evangelist, author, theologian, financier, administrator, and a promoter of missions both at home and abroad. Until he retired as General Secretary-Treasurer of the PAOC in 1932, he was the acknowledged constitutional expert. His colleagues considered him a man with God-given wisdom. Many a thorny issue on the conference floor was solved by his counsel. Apt summary words may be found in Gordon Atter's *Third Force*: "Wherever he went, he left a trail of Pentecostal blessing. From his pen flowed forth a constant stream of Pentecostal literature.... He became a tower of strength in shaping the Canadian Fellowship in its early organization, in its missionary program, and especially in its sound doctrinal development."[12]

Andrew Harvey Argue

The Pentecostal work in Western Canada is forever associated with the name of Andrew Harvey Argue and the city of Winnipeg. He was born in 1868 at Fitzroy Harbor, near Ottawa, the grandson of a Methodist layman who had come to Canada from Ireland in 1821. His father, John, was a Methodist lay preacher who moved his family, which by then included Andrew, to a farm in North Dakota. It was there that Andrew was converted during revival services conducted by the Salvation Army. In those revival meetings, Andrew met a Canadian girl named Eva who had been assisting in the services. They were soon married and began a five-year stint as farmers in North Dakota. The decision by the Argue family to move to Winnipeg was an astute move, for the city was then at the heart of the great economic boom of the Canadian West. Together with his brothers, Andrew launched a successful real estate business.

With a keen interest in gospel work, Andrew often ministered as a Methodist exhorter. While preaching at a camp meeting at Thornbury, Ontario, he came in contact with a written account of what was happening at the Azusa Street meetings. He showed it to American J. H. King of the Fire-Baptized Holiness Church, who was participating in the same camp meeting. King, who would later play a leading role in the Pentecostal Holiness Church, with apparent openness, replied that it "could be possible" that people might speak in unknown tongues. Andrew went back to Winnipeg, learned all he could about the Latter Rain revival, then traveled to Chicago to W. H. Durham's North Avenue Mission. Durham had recently received the baptism in the Holy Spirit in Los Angeles and had turned his Chicago mission into a Pentecostal center. In the "windy city," Andrew sought for the baptism in an atmosphere of excitement and religious phenomena. He later described his experience: "I waited on God for 21 days.... During this time I had a wonderful vision of Jesus.... I was filled with the Holy Ghost, speaking with other tongues as the Spirit gave utterance."[13]

His heart was aflame with this new experience and upon his return to Winnipeg he immediately opened his home for "tarrying meetings." One of his contemporaries, A. G. Ward, stated that through Andrew's influence and ministry "possibly thousands of people in Winnipeg and throughout Manitoba came under the mighty Latter Rain outpouring of the Spirit."[14] When Andrew received his baptism in the Holy Spirit, he was nearly 40 years of age, not a time of life when men usually enter the ministry. Yet he launched a 20-year career as one of the leading Pentecostal evangelists in North America. His experience as a Methodist exhorter, his passion for souls, his supernatural healing (in an A. B. Simpson meeting),[15] and his baptism in the Holy Spirit with tongues-speaking were the basic qualifications he brought to the pulpit. Coupled with these were his natural gifts as a speaker and his platform skills. He stood over six feet in height, was ruggedly handsome, and spoke with a powerful voice and energetic delivery. Gordon Atter described him as "the greatest Pentecostal evangelist Canada produced."[16]

Along with his public preaching ministry Andrew published a paper known as *The Apostolic Messenger*. He printed more than 40,000 copies of some issues, which he distributed across North America. In its pages, Andrew wrote very effectively about the worldwide move of God, citing more than 40 countries where the Pentecostal movement had begun. He also used its pages to defend the Pentecostal doctrines. For example, he discussed the disappearance of the charismata in the Church and cited John Wesley to explain how the gifts could be recovered.[17] It is also significant that Andrew distributed his paper without charge. His financial status was rather unique in that when he sold his real estate business, he was able to invest the proceeds in income-producing property, which allowed him to be financially independent. So wise were his investments that he was able to provide for his own necessities until his death in his 91st year. It was well known that while itinerating as an evangelist, he often gave the "love offering" back to the pastor of some struggling Pentecostal mission.

The concluding comments about A. H. Argue and his immeasurable impact are found in the tribute paid to him by Walter McAlister, who served as General Superintendent of the PAOC 1953-1962. Walter recalled his introduction to the Pentecostal experience under Andrew Argue's ministry in Winnipeg: "I received the Baptism of the Spirit in his mission at 501 Alexander Avenue.... A. H. Argue was a very godly man. As a young boy in his mission I looked up to him as the most saintly man I'd ever seen. His face just seemed to glow with the glory of God."[18]

At the July 1919 Conference in Edmonton, young Walter was ordained for Pentecostal ministry. One of the brethren who laid hands on him in the ordination prayer was the same "godly man," A. H. Argue.

THE PENTECOSTAL ASSEMBLIES OF CANADA

General Superintendents:

George A. Chambers
(1919-1922; 1925-1934)

James Swanson
(1935-1936)

Daniel N. Buntain
(1937-1944)

Campbell B. Smith
(1945-1952)

Walter E. McAlister
(1953-1962)

Tom Johnstone
(1963-1968)

Robert W. Taitinger
(1969-1982)

James M. MacKnight
(1983-1996)

William D. Morrow
(1997-2008)

General Superintendents:

David R. Wells
(2008 to present)

Author:

William A. Griffin
Advisor to the Officers

CHAPTER 18

Pentecostal Assemblies
of Newfoundland
and Labrador

FOUNDER:

Alice B. Garrigus

PENTECOSTAL ASSEMBLIES OF NEWFOUNDLAND AND LABRADOR

By Burton K. Janes [1]

ate in 1910, a diminutive American woman prepared to board the ferry operating between Canada and Newfoundland, a small British colony east of Canada. The step from the pier to the ferry would be a short, albeit momentous, one.

Passing through customs, the official asked her why she was traveling to the island.

"To preach the gospel," she answered.

The surprised official suggested there must be a mistake. Her passport stated she was 52 years old, hardly the age for a career change – especially for a woman in 1910.

The woman responded that she too would have considered the trip a mistake, had not God called her for this very purpose.

We know this woman as Alice Belle Garrigus,[2] the human instrument God used to begin the Pentecostal movement in Newfoundland and Labrador. She is virtually a forgotten Pentecostal pioneer outside her adopted land. But her life, as the founder of what became known as the Pentecostal Assemblies of Newfoundland and Labrador, is an inspiring story of faith in God and determination to fulfill His plan for her at an age when a weaker person might have sought a less strenuous life.

Alice Garrigus, the first child of Lewis and Julia Elizabeth Garrigus, was born on August 2, 1858, in Rockville, a prosperous Connecticut town. Her father was a sash and blind manufacturer.

She had one brother, Albert. The pedigree of the Garrigus name reveals a well-respected family, rich in military honors. Julia Garrigus's illness and early death were traumatic events for her young daughter. So her grandmother took her to Providence, Rhode Island, to live with her.

At 15, the bright teenager began teaching in rural schools. Her small stature initially encouraged bigger students to try to intimidate her. One imposing male, when asked his impression of his new teacher, said, "She is a dreadful little thing, but there is something in her eye which tells me that I guess it wouldn't do to go too far!"[3]

Alice attended Normal School, then spent three years (1878-81) at Mount Holyoke Female Seminary (now Mount Holyoke College), one of America's leading women's seminaries, in South Hadley, Massachusetts. The institution was special to Alice. In 1938, she recalled "those pleasant days spent at college."[4]

Leaving the seminary a year before graduation, she continued her teaching career in Thomaston, Connecticut. At her boardinghouse, she became acquainted with a colleague, Gertrude Wheeler. Their friendship marked the start of Alice's spiritual pilgrimage. Kurt O. Berends wrote: "That journey would take her first within the sphere of the holiness movement and ultimately into Pentecostal circles."[5] Gertrude possessed the born-again experience. "I soon saw the difference between her life and mine," Alice remembered, "and began to seek the Lord very earnestly."[6] Although Alice had been confirmed in the Episcopal Church years before, she remained an inveterate seeker after truth. Her spiritual hunger and restlessness was intensified after she read *The Christian's Secret of a Happy Life* by Hannah Whitall Smith, a lay speaker and author in the American Holiness Movement and the English Higher Life[7] movement. "This I read – often on my knees, eyes blinded with tears – praying fervently: 'O God, if there be such an experience, won't you bring me into it?'"[8]

In June 1888, Alice and Gertrude left on a 10-month

European excursion. Back in the States, the duo received teaching appointments in Bridgeport, Connecticut, and joined the Congregational Church.

The emphases of entire sanctification, Pentecostal terminology, faith ministry, and divine healing were present in local Holiness circles. Alice would eventually enter the Holiness Movement, and later the Pentecostal Movement.

Gertrude began attending a mission located in one of the worst sections of Bridgeport. Alice tried unsuccessfully to dissuade her friend from associating with the "down-and-out." Eventually, out of curiosity and laying aside her pride, Alice attended a single meeting, "just to see how drunkards got saved,"[9] she was quick to add.

The mission leader, William D. Fowler who, with his wife, would later travel to Newfoundland with Alice, spoke on "absolute surrender, the way to victorious life."[10] Alice listened attentively and went forward for prayer, a life-changing experience. "The consecration was deep and thorough," she later testified, "and the Spirit witnessed to it."[11]

Around 1893, Alice discontinued her teaching career to work full time in Beulah Mission Home, a faith venture which had been founded by Gertrude for destitute women and children, located in one of the town's better neighborhoods. Alice and Gertrude operated the home for six years, at which time Alice felt divinely led to work "among the saloons and dives."[12]

Alice returned to the Fowlers. In 1900, she moved in with them above their mission, an arrangement lasting three years.

In 1904, Alice traveled to Rumney, New Hampshire, where she contacted the First Fruit Harvesters Association (now The New England Fellowship of Evangelicals). Joel Adams Wright founded this interdenominational organization in 1897 to "strengthen the churches and send missionaries to the end of the earth."[13] It looked for workers who would accept the Bible as their creed, allow the Holy Spirit to lead them and conduct meetings from town to town. Kurt Berends observed that Alice "entered the ministry as an experienced holiness practitioner, able to lead services and guide others towards the 'higher life.'"[14] She spent six years (1904-10) as an itinerant preacher with the organization.

In 1905, Alice began hearing about the Welsh Revival and, a year later, the Azusa Street Revival in Los Angeles, California. "Had it been possible," she declared, "I, too, like many others, would have wended my way to old Azusa Street. As that was impossible, I began most earnestly, with prayer and fasting, to seek for the experience [God] was giving His people."[15] She termed that experience "the Pentecostal-fulness."[16]

Around 1907, Alice attended a Christian and Missionary Alliance convention in Old Orchard, Maine. Several determined seekers remained at the conclusion of the meetings. Frank Bartleman, an unofficial chronicler of the infant Pentecostal Movement, arrived on the grounds but, according to Alice's memoirs, encountered stiff resistance from denominational leaders. Not surprisingly, though, the lingering believers welcomed him. "While we were seated on the ground," Alice recalled more than three decades later, "he stood for hours, telling us the deeper things of God."[17]

Following Bartleman's departure, the seekers met in a dilapidated barn. Alice remembered the event: "What a gathering it was – all coming with one purpose, 'to tarry until.' Missionaries, ministers, Christian workers, the rich and the poor, all down on their faces in the hay, pleading for the 'Promise of the Father.' It was an individual matter, each after his full inheritance.... The Comforter had come and set His seal upon each yielded life, speaking for Himself in any language He pleased."[18] Alice was among the recipients of the Pentecostal baptism.

In October 1908, while staying with minister-friends at Rumney, a stranger approached Alice. She instinctively knew God had a message for her and thought immediately of China. The woman stated that Alice was looking too far. "Then followed a message in tongues," Alice wrote, "and the word, 'NEWFOUNDLAND,' came forth."[19] Jumping from her chair, Alice danced and praised God. The stranger added that Alice would leave in November, her fare would be provided, she would dearly love the people, and others would follow her.

Alice's immediate thought was, "What and where is Newfoundland?" She consulted a map. "From the hour God called," she later confessed, "my heart was in N[ew]f[ound]l[an]d."[20] Although her exodus to Newfoundland was not immediate, she learned as much as possible about her future home.

On December 1, 1910, Alice, accompanied by the Fowlers, arrived in St. John's, under the auspices of the First Fruit Harvesters Association. God had impressed upon her His desire for a mission in Newfoundland's capital city. They were a veritable Christmas gift for the island!

The trio rented and renovated a building downtown. On Easter Sunday, April 16, 1911, they conducted their first Pentecostal service at the storefront "Bethesda Mission." Alice's preaching centered on conversion, adult water baptism, the baptism in the Holy Spirit with the physical evidence of speaking in tongues, and the imminent return of Christ. In the words of James A. Hewitt, "Her Full Gospel message always emphasized the subjective element of the faith but never with a hint of religious fanaticism or at the expense of personal decorum. Garrigus was a leader strong enough to control any fanatics yet sufficiently pliable to yield to the Spirit's work."[21]

Alice's nearly 40 years in Newfoundland were very busy. She opened Bethesda Mission in St. John's, Newfoundland, on Easter Sunday 1911. She served as evangelist in charge of Bethesda Mission and held several denominational executive positions. She traveled frequently to assemblies, reporting on their progress and offering encouragement. And she wrote a corpus of letters, articles, sermons and memoirs. In 1942, at 84 years of age, she relocated to scenic Clarke's Beach, about 50 miles from St. John's. There she lived in a modest dwelling – "Rehoboth," a biblical name meaning broad places – until her death in 1949 at 91.

The movement expanded outside the capital city after 1920 and was registered with the government as a denomination in 1925. It spread to Labrador in the early 1930s with the aid of the *Gospel Messenger*. The denomination developed independently of The Pentecostal Assemblies of Canada but shares a common statement of faith and works closely in overseas missions.

Joseph R. Smallwood, Premier of Newfoundland and Labrador from 1949 to 1972, referred to Bethesda Mission as a "small acorn," from which "Pentecostalism in Newfoundland has grown into a sturdy oak."[22]

Pentecostal Assemblies of Newfoundland and Labrador

General Superintendents:

Robert C. English
(1925-1927)

Eugene Vaters
(1927-1962)

A. Stanley Bursey
(1962-1980)

Roy D. King
(1980-1996)

A. Earl Batstone
(1996-2002)

H. Paul Foster
(2002 to present)

Author:

Burton K. Janes
Former Managing Editor, Good Tidings

CHAPTER 19

Pentecostal Church
of God

FOUNDERS:

George C. Brinkman

John C. Sinclair

PREPARING THE WAY FOR THE PENTECOSTAL CHURCH OF GOD:
George Brinkman and John Sinclair

By Aaron M. Wilson and Wayman C. Ming

ooking back nearly a century ago, it is difficult to understand the importance of publications to the formation and spread of the early twentieth century Pentecostal revival. In his book *Heaven Below*, Grant Wacker states, "Periodicals constituted by far the most important technique for sustaining national and world consciousness. They created the impression that Pentecostals were triumphing everywhere. Holy Ghost papers routinely published long lists of approved – and sometimes disapproved – evangelists, churches, camps, books, and even other periodicals."[1] While other early Pentecostal organizations grew out of a variety of felt needs, the Pentecostal Church of God can trace its inception directly to a publication and its owner and editor, George C. Brinkman and his wife, Clara.

George C. Brinkman

George Cecil Brinkman was born in Little Orleans, Maryland, on July 17, 1879.[2] As a young man he was employed by the railroad as a stenographer. It was this job that launched his interest in printing.[3] Through the ministry of William Piper, who was instrumental in organizing the Stone Church in Chicago, George Brinkman enthusiastically accepted the Pentecostal message and later became the pastor of the Pentecostal Herald Mission, located at 6648 Halsted Street in Chicago.[4]

Clara Brinkman, like her husband, was devoted to spreading the gospel. A letter written by Alpha D. McClure, a well known evangelist, describes the Brinkmans in this manner: "We found Brother and Sister Brinkman very precious people with lives wholly given to this work. It was an inspiration to see their faithfulness and how Sister Brinkman goes to the office every day with their nine-month-old baby, sacrificing the comforts of home to help spread the gospel of the Kingdom."[5] Unfortunately, the Brinkman's daughter, little Sarah, contracted pneumonia shortly after and passed away.

Although George Brinkman was a preacher and pastor, he was first and foremost a publisher. He had written tracts and articles for other publications and in 1915 began publication of *The Pentecostal Herald*. His paper soon grew to be the largest circulation among the Pentecostal periodicals at one time. The April 1918 issue of the paper reported an annual circulation of 550,000.

The October 1919 issue was of particular interest. In it appeared a revival report from Elton, Wisconsin, where over 100 people were saved. The evangelists were Charles Vanderploeg and his wife, and Alpha McClure. The same issue aired a grievance between the editor, George Brinkman, and the Assemblies of God. Although Brinkman was never credentialed by the Assemblies of God, he had numerous ties with the denomination, and according to Brinkman, referred over 200 ministers and evangelists to the Assemblies of God for credentials between 1914 and 1919.[6]

The grievance quoted minister friends who stated that Brother J. W. Welch, Chairman of the Assemblies of God, had discouraged their churches from taking the paper, recommending instead that they be loyal to what had become their denomination's paper, *The Christian Evangel* (soon to be renamed *The Pentecostal Evangel*).

Eli DePriest, one of the founding members of the Pentecostal Church of God recorded:

> *Then came time for the meeting of a little group of men on State Street in Chicago. Fervent prayers went up to God in this meeting and the place was shaken. Here the Pentecostal Church*

*of God of America came into existence. Rev. George Brinkman
was the printer of the literature for this new movement. Rev.
John Sinclair was the General Superintendent. Rev. Bell was
Treasurer.*[7]

The movement was established under the name The Pentecostal
Assemblies of the U.S.A. With the substantial involvement
of Canadian R. E. McAlister, there was discussion to the effect
that *The Pentecostal Herald* might be the publication for both the
Pentecostal Assemblies of Canada and the United States movement
with the same basic name. McAlister's involvement in the Jesus
Name controversy appears to have prevented further exploration
on that front.

George Brinkman was called to his heavenly home on July 10,
1960, while reciting the Twenty-Third Psalm in his son David's arms.
Brinkman's sons, David and Samuel, continued the family printing
business. When David retired in 1991, he donated the printing
equipment to the Illinois District Council of the Assemblies of
God in Carlinville, a fitting place of rest for the historic presses
that were such a powerful voice of the early Pentecostal revival.[8]

John C. Sinclair

The first chairman of the Pentecostal Church of God was a
noted Chicago minister and pastor, John Chalmers Sinclair. John
had been a part of the formation of the Assemblies of God in 1914,
but withdrew when they adopted a doctrinal statement concerning
the Oneness doctrine referred to as the "New Issue" in 1916.

John Sinclair was born on August 29, 1862, in Lybster, Scotland,
a small but industrious fishing village on the northeastern coast
of the Scottish Highlands.[9] When he was in his early twenties he
immigrated to the United States and became a citizen in 1893.

John was reputed to be the first person in Chicago to receive the
Pentecostal experience with the evidence of tongues. He is reported
as saying, "The saints at 328 West 63rd Street began to pray on the

first of July 1906 that God would baptize us in the Holy Ghost, as we had heard that the saints at Los Angeles had been baptized." On November 19, 1906, a Pentecostal revival began in his church and continued for a number of months.

A popular speaker, John preached the Pentecostal message in churches and conventions. Perhaps the best description of John Sinclair came from Rev. E. N. Bell:

> *"I have never had Sinclair take the attitude of a learner, but he wants to do all the talking and all the teaching, and assumes from start to finish the attitude of one thoroughly capable of teaching the other fellow. Yet this is part of the whole makeup, rather than the egotism that might be supposed from the same attitude in another man. One would have to know Sinclair to be able to see that he is not really egotistical as his manner makes him appear. He is naturally quick in thought and speech, and naturally takes the lead."*[10]

Early in 1923, John Sinclair obtained his credentials with the Assemblies of God, but by the summer of 1926, he had ceased to be active in the full-time ministry, retiring to a farm he owned in the small community of Union Mills, Indiana. After a three-year illness and suffering from hypertension, arteriosclerosis and a blood clot on his lung, John died on February 27, 1936.[11]

The end of Sinclair's ministry closed an important chapter in the life of an extraordinary man who was privileged to participate in the formation of two Pentecostal denominations – the Pentecostal Church of God and Assemblies of God.

Historical Overview

The organization now known as the Pentecostal Church of God was founded in 1919. The 1920 convention featured John G. Lake, internationally known evangelist and minister. Reports of healings and operation of the gifts of the Spirit were given. Lake was not a member of the denomination until some years later when he served as Assistant General Superintendent for the Northwest District.[12]

In 1922 the name was changed from the Pentecostal Assemblies of the USA to the Pentecostal Church of God. However, when the overseeing leadership found the name already registered, they added "of America" to the name to obtain some uniqueness. In 1979, the words "of America" were once again dropped, returning the movement to the 1922 name, Pentecostal Church of God.[13]

Because of the lack of full-time leadership, the early leaders under the title of Moderator, and later, General Superintendent, also served as pastors of local churches. It was not until the election of Rik Field in 1926 that an evangelist was chosen who could travel the nation and give a national leadership scope to the organization.[14]

With the election of Alpha D. McClure as national leader in 1931 the headquarters were moved to Ottumwa, Iowa, where Alpha continued to serve as a pastor. The McClures also began a magazine, *The Pentecostal Messenger*, which succeeded *The Pentecostal Herald* as the official publication of the movement.[15]

Two significant considerations were formative in the early years of the Pentecostal Church of God. The first consideration involved the recognition of God's call on women. Ida Tribett, who served as a national evangelist for the movement for several years, was the very first person ordained by the Pentecostal Church of God.[16]

The second consideration involved the inclusion of African Americans. The third general convention of the movement was shared with the Church of God in Christ. C. H. Mason, head of Church of God in Christ, was the principal speaker. While no merger resulted, there was a sentiment that they were "almost perfectly agreed on all points of doctrine, and it was agreed that the two bodies should cooperate in every way possible."[17]

PENTECOSTAL CHURCH OF GOD

First Moderator:

John C. Sinclair
(1919-1921)

Moderators:

Edward Matthews
(1921-1922)

John B. Huffman
(1922-1923)

S. W. Shepherd
(1923-1925)

Osborn V. Gilliland
(1925-1926)

Rik Field
(1926-1931)

A. D. McClure
(1931-1933)

G. F. C. Fons
(1933-1935)

General Superintendents:

M. D. Townsend
(1935-1937)

Harold M. Collins
(1937-1942)

J. W. May
(1942-1947)

H. T. Owens
(1947-1949)

M. F. Coughran
(1949-1953)

R. Dennis Heard
(1953-1975)

Roy M. Chappell
(1975-1987)

James D. Gee
(1987-2001)

Phil L. Redding
(2001-2005)

General Bishops:

Charles R. Mosier
(2005-2006)

Charles G. Scott
(2007 to present)

Authors:

Aaron M. Wilson
Historian

Wayman C. Ming
General Secretary

CHAPTER 20

Pentecostal
Free Will Baptist

FOUNDER:

Herbert F. Carter

PERSEVERANCE PAVES THE WAY FOR THE PFWB:
Herbert Carter

By Herbert Carter

D r. Herbert F. Carter was born June 20, 1933, to Arby H. Carter and Betty Lockerman Carter. He was the ninth of twelve children, nine boys and three girls. His father was a bi-vocational pastor, also working as a paint contractor. Arby did all the preaching and pastoring with the family tagging along. The older children helped paint or tend the farm while the younger ones picked cotton, gathered corn, or fed the animals.

One Saturday night at a youth camp meeting, 16-year-old Herbert heard the preacher ask, "What will you do with Jesus?" in the title of his sermon. As Lois Blanton and Jetty Parker led him in a simple prayer he bowed at his pew, saying, "I can, I will, and I do believe that Jesus saves me now." Three years later, he was elected director of the youth camp meeting at the same location where he was converted.

Back at public school in Clinton, North Carolina, others noticed a change in the young man. He was asked to read scripture and pray in chapel and served as his class chaplain. After the family moved to Wallace, North Carolina, young Herbert also taught a Sunday school class in his father's church and served as a youth leader and director of Vacation Bible School.

Herbert went on to Holmes Bible College, and then transferred to William Carter College and Evangelical Theological Seminary in Goldsboro, North Carolina, established by his first cousin, Dr.

William Howard Carter. During this time, Herbert held revivals in local churches, preached for his cousin at Edgewood Evangelical Baptist Church, and spoke frequently on the *Quiet Hour* broadcast, a radio ministry aired on multiple stations in eastern North Carolina.

While in college, Herbert met a beautiful young lady, Mary Key, from Portsmouth, Virginia. After graduation, they were married at Falcon, North Carolina, where she worked at Falcon Orphanage. God blessed this union with two wonderful boys.

After graduation, Herbert was invited to be pastor of Stoney Run Church, the denomination's flagship church, established in 1850. The invitation came after Herbert preached a ten-day revival there, with many converted or receiving deeper life experiences. Then in 1959, after just three years and ten months in the pulpit, he was asked to be superintendent of the Pentecostal Free Will Baptist Church, Inc. (PFWB). He was only 25.

PFWB

The PFWB denomination is headquartered in Dunn, North Carolina, site of the Azusa Street East Revival. It actually traces its roots back to colonial times. In 1727, a preacher named Paul Palmer helped found the state's first Free or General Baptist congregation in northeastern North Carolina. From that beginning, a collection of Free Will Baptist churches spread, eventually forming regional conferences.

The denomination was formed on April 28, 1959, from the merger of three of those conferences. The oldest was the Cape Fear Conference of Free Will Baptists, formed in 1855. Also included were the Wilmington Conference of Free Will Baptists, formed in 1908, and the New River Conference of Free Will Baptists.

PFWB's Pentecostal heritage dates back to New Year's Eve, 1906, when Gaston B. Cashwell, returning from a visit to the Azusa Street Revival in California, began preaching in Dunn. In the ensuing three-week revival, a number of Free Will Baptist leaders were baptized in the Holy Spirit and later led their churches to embrace the experience as doctrine, along with sanctification as a second, definite work of grace.

Herbert was secretary of the Wilmington conference. When the loosely allied conferences of Free Will Baptists began to unravel, he asked their leaders to consider combining all their churches under one charter, constitution, and set of by-laws. They agreed. Within days, an attorney drew up the appropriate paperwork and set matters in motion. The constitution and by-laws followed, written by the Secretary, A. B. Dawsey; Assistant Superintendent, J. E. Andrews; Treasurer, J. Edward Johnson; and Dr. Carter.

Executive committees of the three conferences became the General Board of Directors. A few months later, the new denomination's first general conference took place in Clinton, North Carolina, and ministry credentials were presented to all classifications of the ministers in the group.

Herbert recalls how he felt as a young man just out of college, with only three years and ten months of pastoral experience, suddenly called to shoulder such a heavy burden. "It appeared enormously overwhelming. It was staggering to consider what was ahead." When he arrived home and broke the news to his wife, Mary, both responded with tears.

There were plenty of obstacles and few resources. Money, equipment, and procedures all were in short supply. The combined treasury provided only a few dollars and that was soon gone. A number of times, the bank account dropped below $200, with no savings to draw on. The denomination first attempted to raise money by asking six dollars of each church member per year, then switched to a tithing program.

The office inherited one old Underwood typewriter, a Speed-O-Print mimeograph, and a couple of reams of paper. There was not a single desk or filing cabinet. The new board members operated out of their personal brief cases. Everything you can imagine needed in an office had to be provided, including the office itself.

Problems were numerous. Despite the desire for unity, suspicion, doubt, and fear were the order of the day. Threats of churches withdrawing poured into the office, and rumors circulated, causing further pain and conflict. Of the original 129 churches in the three conferences, 93 churches remained with doors open and regular meetings.

Though the old alliance of Free Will Baptist churches had no central power and preserved the inherent rights of each member conference, it was largely responsible for the radical restructuring that took place in the PFWB denomination. Ironically, it was the unraveling of that alliance, rather than its growth and development that resulted in consolidation and centralization.

What followed, Herbert recalls, was like digging a footing for a new house, with hours of laborious work stretching ahead before a structure could rise. The new denomination was divided into seven districts, allowing for an equal distribution of churches. On a large map, boundaries were drawn and districts named. Long-overdue quarterly meetings were scheduled.

Beyond that, much work needed to be done. There were meetings to arrange and churches to notify about dates, times, and financial responsibilities. There were speakers to engage for a July camp meeting and a promotion to design and mail. There was an annual conference to organize and a keynote address to prepare. At the same time, Herbert was building his own house in Clinton, North Carolina, and facing the task of moving.

Perhaps the most troubling problem facing the denomination was its orphanage in Dunn, which housed 16 children. It came with a debt of $38,000. Its provisional license was about to expire, with state regulators requiring almost $50,000 in repairs. In a special session in early 1961, leaders urged the denomination to close the orphanage, a move that brought more pain and conflict. Ultimately, all the children were placed in other child care facilities.

Heritage Bible College

In 1971, Herbert called the Board of Directors to discuss the need for a Bible college to educate ministers and lay people, a burden he shared with Assistant General Superintendent Dr. Ned Sauls. The Board voted by a great majority to launch a four-year, co-educational institution and named O. Talmadge Spence as president. That fall, Heritage Bible College opened its doors, occupying the buildings formerly used by the orphanage.

Now a fully accredited college, Heritage has graduated hundreds of students to spread the gospel to the world. On its grounds stands a monument commemorating the Azusa Street East Revival, which was held in a tobacco processing plant on the corner of East Layton and Pope Streets in the nearby town of Dunn, North Carolina. The revival spread to other parts of the Southeast, paving the way for this denomination and changing the region's religious landscape.

Still Going Strong

Over the years, Herbert continued his education. He earned masters and doctoral degrees in divinity from what was then Luther Rice Seminary. He also received his doctorate in theology from Fuller Theological Seminary in Pasadena, California, concentrating in missions, evangelism, and church growth.

After stepping down as superintendent in 1984, Herbert continued at the denominational headquarters in the position of World Missions Director, continuing to preach around the nation and world. Afterwards, he served for seven years of pastoral leadership in North Haven Church. Dr. Carter accepted the roles of executive vice president and academic dean of Heritage Bible College, where he also teaches theology, church growth, and the Book of Revelation.

He and his wife, Mary, are members of the historic Stoney Run Church, his first pastorate, but attend their son's church in Rolesville, North Carolina, where they enjoy seeing their whole family active in Christian service.

The denomination has come a long way from the early years when there were 93 churches, mostly small, and only 5,000 members in a radius of about 100 miles, with no major ministries in place to enhance their growth. PFWB is concentrated in eastern North Carolina, South Carolina, Virginia, Pennsylvania, and Florida with missions in Mexico, Central America, South America, and the Philippines, Puerto Rico, Africa, and several other locations. Besides a Bible college, PFWB now operates Blessings Bookstore and Crusader Youth Camp and publishes the *Messenger*, a bimonthly magazine.

Fifty years after the denomination was founded, Herbert looks back with pride on what was accomplished – challenges, conflicts, and all. He stated, "It is just the honest story of where we were and what has happened, in part, on our journey. If we had it to do over we would do it again!"

Dr. Herbert Carter believes the Pentecostal Free Will Baptist Church is positioned to experience the greatest growth in all of its history.

PENTECOSTAL FREE WILL BAPTIST

Superintendents:

Herbert F. Carter
(1959–1984)

Don Sauls
(1984–1996)

Preston Heath
(1996 to present)

Author:

Herbert F. Carter

CHAPTER 21

Pentecostal Holiness Church *of* Canada

FOUNDER:

Joseph H. King

CONTINUING THE BOOK OF ACTS:
Joseph H. King

By Gordon McDonald

The Pentecostal Holiness Church of Canada is in reality a continuation of the dynamic first century missionary church, which was born on the day of Pentecost. It is also part of the great Pentecostal revival at the turn of the twentieth century, resulting in the appearance of several dozen holiness and Pentecostal denominations.

One of the first groups to officially designate itself as a member of the "Pentecostal" movement was the Pentecostal Holiness Church, with its roots in the mid-western and southeastern United States. From the very beginning, the Pentecostal Holiness Church has played a significant role within this movement.

The unique character of the Pentecostal Holiness Church is seen in its very name, which places it astride two major revival movements: the holiness revival of the late nineteenth century, and the Pentecostal revival of the twentieth century. It has attempted to preserve the best of the Wesleyan tradition while perpetuating the best in the Pentecostal tradition.

In 1898 at Goldsboro, North Carolina, the Pentecostal Holiness Church came into being. A general superintendent and other officials were elected and conferences were held annually. In August of 1898, at Anderson, South Carolina, the Fire-Baptized Holiness Association was also born. In 1902 the name was changed from the Fire-Baptized Holiness Association to the Fire-Baptized

Holiness Church. A strong feeling emerged among the members of both the Pentecostal Holiness Church and the Fire-Baptized Holiness Church that the two should unite. Both were preaching the same biblical truths. On January 30, 1911, at Falcon, North Carolina, delegates from both groups met for the purpose of effecting consolidation of the two bodies. The two groups officially merged the next day. The name "Pentecostal Holiness Church" was adopted for the consolidated organization.

The Pentecostal Holiness Church had its beginning in Canada in the 1920s and was incorporated in the province of Ontario on May 7, 1928. The founding conference was conducted by Bishop J.H. King.

Joseph Hillery King was born August 11, 1869, in Rockmill Township, Anderson County, South Carolina. Joseph's father was a sharecropper and the family lived in hovels, with each family member working hard from an early age. The family rarely attended church due to the heavy workload and to a scarcity of pastors.

William Asbury Dodge conducted a camp meeting near Joseph King's home on August 11, 1885. Joseph was among those who came to the altar for salvation. Having turned 16 years old on this same day, he would later refer to the date as his double birthday. Joseph joined the Methodist Episcopal church (South) on August 17, 1885, and became licensed in 1890. He remained committed to the holiness wing of Methodism, a position from which many Methodists had departed. He believed he was sanctified in the experience he called fire-baptism.

After more schooling and years of ministry, Joseph was elected Assistant Secretary of the Annual Conference. When he left the Annual Conference in 1897 to take charge of the Simpson Circuit in Northeastern Georgia, he was 28 years old. He was a graduate of the School of Theology, a fully ordained minister of the Methodist Episcopal Church, Assistant Secretary of his Conference, and a member of the Examining Committee.

In 1898 Joseph attended services in Royston, Georgia, led

by Benjamin Harden Irwin, who had founded his Fire Baptized Holiness Associations in the southern states. When Irwin called the various state associations together to form a national organization, Joseph King left the Methodist church and joined Irwin's Fire-Baptized Holiness Church (FBHC).

After preaching "fire-baptism" in various meetings, Joseph left Royston for a new pastorate in Toronto, Canada. Late in 1899 he received a letter from Benjamin Irwin, asking Joseph to come to Lincoln, Nebraska, to be the assistant editor of the church's paper, *Live Coals of Fire*.

When Irwin confessed to moral failure in 1900 Joseph was unanimously elected as the new General Overseer of the FBHC. Over the next few years he traveled and preached throughout the U.S. and Canada, trying to heal the wounds of Irwin's fall and consolidate the church's functions.

In September 1906 A. H. Argue told Joseph about the new Azusa Street revival. Though Joseph had renounced the doctrine of a subsequent fire-baptism, he was still open to the idea of Spirit baptism subsequent to sanctification.

Gaston Cashwell, a minister of the Holiness Church of North Carolina, promoted this "new" doctrine, after experiencing a Spirit baptism at Azusa Street, in which he spoke in tongues. When Gaston returned to North Carolina, he began a meeting in Dunn on December 31, 1906. This revival continued through January 1907 and heavily influenced the Fire-Baptized Holiness Church. Members of the congregation in Toccoa, Georgia, where Joseph was technically serving as interim pastor, were present at the Dunn meetings. When he returned from Canada these folks presented this "new" message to Joseph.

Joseph opposed the new teaching both publicly and privately. As editor of *Live Coals*, Joseph published a lengthy article by J. Hudson Ballard which used scripture to refute this doctrinal innovation. Joseph was bothered with the insistence of the necessity of speaking in tongues as the exclusive evidence of Spirit baptism.

Despite these doctrinal reservations, Joseph was open to an experience of Spirit baptism but hardly as a shallow follower. On February 14, 1907, Joseph secluded himself in order to study the controversy, beginning with Dean Alford's commentary based on the New Testament Greek text. Joseph was stunned. Alford indicated that tongues were not expressly mentioned in all of the Acts account of Spirit baptism, but tongues were definitely implied according to the Greek text. Further study and prayer on this point from other commentaries led Joseph to reject all of his own previous arguments.

He began to pray and seek in earnest this new experience. He slept little that night, and the next day continued to fast and to pray. At an afternoon service on February 15, 1907, Joseph received his Spirit baptism and spoke in tongues.

Rushing to Royston, Joseph King informed other leaders of the Fire-Baptized Holiness Church of the change in his doctrinal position and of his own experience. This explanation took the entire night of February 15, 1907. On the following morning, these men accepted Joseph's explanation and went to Toccoa themselves in order to seek this experience. Cashwell was then invited to conduct further services in Royston, which was accomplished in March.

The following year in Anderson, South Carolina, at the General Convention of the Fire-Baptized Church, the Articles of Faith were officially changed to reflect the new doctrine and experience. King would preach and teach this understanding of Spirit baptism until his death in 1946.

Canada's Western Canada Conference (originally called the British Columbia Conference) was formed in 1943 under the leadership of Rev. Harold Paul. The Maritime Conference was established in Halifax, Nova Scotia, in 1944 and was conducted by Bishop Dan T. Muse. Through the years the influence of the Pentecostal Holiness Church has spread in Canada by the establishing of local churches in the provinces of Alberta, British Columbia, New Brunswick, Nova Scotia, Ontario, Quebec, and Manitoba.

Letters Patent incorporating the Pentecostal Holiness Church of Canada under a Dominion Charter, dated April 27, 1971, were secured. The First General Conference convened on May 25, 1971, at Toronto, Ontario. Dr. G. H. Nunn was elected to serve as the first general superintendent of this newly formed Canadian Church. He was re-elected at each subsequent conference until his resignation in 1991. At that time Wayne Longard was elected as the General Superintendent by the General Board of Administration to complete that term. He was re-elected during the session of the Seventh General Conference held in Vancouver, BC, in 1994 to serve for another four-year term.

After Wayne Longard passed away in January of 1997, Dr. Gordon McDonald was elected as General Superintendent at a metting of the General Board of Administration on April 19, 1997. He was re-elected to that position on July 18, 1998, to serve for the next four-year term. Gordon McDonald was re-elected on July 11, 2002, for another four-year term.

Pentecostal Holiness Church of Canada

General Superintendents:

G. H. Nunn
(1971–1991)

Wayne Longard
(1991–1997)

Superintendent and Author:

Gordon McDonald
(1997 to present)

CHAPTER 22

United Holy Church
of America, Inc.

FOUNDER:

Henry Lee Fisher

THE RISE OF THE UNITED HOLY CHURCH OF AMERICA, INC.:
Bishop Henry Lee Fisher

By Dennis Ball

The United Holy Church of America, Inc. came into existence as an outgrowth of a holiness prayer meeting held in Method, North Carolina, on the first Sunday of May in 1886.[1] This meeting was conducted by Rev. Isaac Cheshier in a private home. Though attended by both men and women, the other leading men present were Rev. L. M. Mason, Rev. Henry C. Snipes, and G. A. Mials. This small, seemingly insignificant cottage meeting was, in fact, a manifestation of the holiness revival that was sweeping the entire country. Primarily a Methodist-led spiritual renewal that was attempting to restore the vitality of the Wesleyan teaching and experience of "entire sanctification," this movement gave birth to several new holiness denominations.[2]

In November 1892, the group out of Method was still a very loosely connected fellowship of ministers of the gospel, missions, and small churches. These ministers carried the message of their holiness experience to Wilmington, North Carolina, in an organized revival meeting. There Henry Lee Fisher, who had obtained permission to move to Wilmington to help financially support his family back in Salisbury, was deeply and radically transformed by what he described as a "newfound experience of holiness."[3] His encounter with God, which he often called "the Holy Fire," filled him with joy he had never known before. Even after 30 years, Henry recalled the event with deep feeling and emotion in his personal diary: "This is my spiritual birthday, 30 years in Holiness. The glory is all His. Amen."[4]

Henry estimated he was about eighteen years old at the time of this experience. However, a census taker visiting the family home in Salisbury, North Carolina, in 1880 was informed that the young boy in the home, named Henry, was three years old.[5] Based on these official government records, Henry was actually fifteen years old in 1892. It is clear, then, he was extremely young when he had his first defining spiritual experience. He was certainly a young man of unusual seriousness, devotion, and spiritual commitment for his years.

The issue of Henry's youth highlights the very early age at which he assumed responsibility and leadership in the fledgling church organization. He was ordained in 1900 and worked zealously as an evangelist throughout North Carolina and Virginia. By 1905 he was called to and assumed the pastorate of two churches. In 1907, at the age of thirty, he was elected to the office of the General Superintendent of Sunday Schools for the organization. Only nine years later H. L. Fisher was elected president of the entire church.[6] As president, Henry Lee Fisher, in essence, became the overseer and presiding bishop. The rapid rise at such a young age to the hierarchy and leadership of the church distinguishes Henry as a young black man who was viewed as capable, mature, serious in purpose, able to lead, wise beyond his years, and sound in the faith.

H. L. Fisher served 31 years as presiding bishop. At his demise in 1947 he was the moving force in expanding the church into twenty additional states and four foreign countries. Under his leadership, the single convocation of churches that had begun in Durham, North Carolina, at the close of the nineteenth century was used as a platform to intentionally establish nine additional convocations. These regional gatherings of local churches stretched from Bermuda in the North Atlantic to California on the Pacific Ocean. District Convocations were operating as far north as the New England states and south in the Caribbean island of Barbados. Across the Atlantic, in Liberia, West Africa, mission stations were working under the organization's banner. During Henry's tenure, the church ceased to be primarily an eastern North Carolina phenomenon and took on a national and international character. It is remarkable that in 1918, 70 churches are listed as belonging to the single Convocation that existed at that time.[7] By 1948, six months after the death of Fisher, the official yearbook lists 205 churches as members of the original Convocation in North Carolina. It also shows 352 churches as part of the nine existing Convocations.[8] Undeniably, by the time of his death in 1947, the church that Henry Fisher inherited in 1916 had undergone a radical transformation.

A close examination and analysis of the life and writings of Henry Fisher and the United Holy Church reveal that the potent force behind the organization's dynamic growth was a spirituality that was both Wesleyan and Pentecostal. Henry's spiritual life and practice, and certainly that of the organization, were shaped by his "experience of holiness," which he clearly understood to be a definite work of the Holy Spirit. His journals show him to be a man of deep spirituality who constantly prayed for the empowering and transforming presence of the Holy Spirit in his life and ministry. It was because of such encounters with the Holy Spirit and his subsequent testimony of this experience that Henry Fisher, along with a multitude of others during that period, were forced out of their churches and compelled to start new denominations.[9] Further, Henry understood in the Wesleyan mold that God had "thrust them out" of their former churches for the specific purpose of spreading "holiness" teaching throughout the world.[10] In one of his first annual reports to the church as president, he urged, "In our zeal we must ever keep uppermost in our minds the purpose for which God thrust us out: that is to spread Bible Holiness over these lands and to the regions beyond."[11] Thus, Henry understood the holiness experience to be determinative not only for his life and ministry, but also for the life and ministry of the church.

As a consequence, Henry developed a strong drive to engage in missions and evangelistic work at home and abroad. His deep sense of mission produced an aggressive, intentional, and robust strategy to expand the borders of the organization and spread the message of "Bible Holiness." He traveled regularly and widely throughout the country. His zealous efforts as a traveling evangelist contributed to one of the most significant changes in the early years of the denomination. In particular, Henry's fruitful evangelistic exploits in Virginia during the years leading up to 1905 prompted the early leaders, by 1909, to change the name of the organization from "Holy Church of North Carolina" to "Holy Church of North Carolina and Virginia."[12] Besides this, through Henry's passionate and diligent preaching on the streets of Durham, North Carolina, five additional congregations were planted and organized in and around that city.

Bishop Fisher's strong support for missions was providentially cemented by a vision he had while attending a Christian and Missionary Alliance convention in Cleveland, Ohio, in 1916. He saw "the world lost in heathen darkness and we, as a church, were responsible to God to give them the light of the Gospel."[13] This spiritual encounter actually enlarged his vision and placed in his spirit a stronger personal obligation and sense of urgency to give for the sake of others. Three months later, Henry was elected president of the church at its Annual Convocation. One of his first acts as president, in response to his vision in Cleveland, was to initiate another change in the name of the church from "Holy Church of North Carolina and Virginia" to the "United Holy Church of America, Inc." The church was formally incorporated under this new name in 1918. His stated goal was "to operate in every state of the Union, the isles of the sea, and every country in the world."[14]

At this point in 1916, the church did not have a foreign mission board or foreign missions or missionaries. Nevertheless, in 1917, Bishop Fisher, as the leading officer of a predominantly African-American church during the midst of World War I, raised

$100 at the Annual Convocation and sent it to the Christian and Missionary Alliance headquarters in New York.[15] He raised another $90 at his local congregation in Durham, North Carolina, and also sent that gift to the Christian and Missionary Alliance headquarters to support foreign mission work.[16] This is remarkable in light of the fact that many in the African-American community were enduring personal hardship because of the war. Henry gave liberally and unselfishly toward foreign missions irrespective of whom or what church organization might receive credit. In 1918, at Henry's urging, a General Mission Board was established. In 1920 he personally escorted the church's first two foreign missionaries, Annie and Isaac Williams, to the docks in New York, where they sailed to Liberia, West Africa. His personal diaries reflect a voluminous daily correspondence with a multitude of persons in and outside of the United Holy Church. Despite his busy schedule and the amount of correspondence, Henry made time to correspond regularly with the church's missionaries in Liberia and Barbados.

Henry's spirituality was clearly Wesleyan and Pentecostal. The experience of holiness was the essence of the gospel. Nothing was more important for understanding, living, and proclaiming the gospel. In the first *Manual of Faith and Discipline* adopted by the church in 1910, produced solely by his own effort, Henry declared boldly, "The experience of holiness or Christian perfection is the mainspring of all gospel truth."[17] He saw the experience of holiness as vital in "apostolic times" and possessed by the "apostolic church." For Henry this experience was so identified with the apostles that he called it "apostolic holiness" or "Bible holiness."[18] He revised the 1910 *Manual*, formally articulating a definitive Pentecostal article of faith, which had previously been assumed. His revisions, adopted in 1912, stated, "We believe in the baptism of the Holy Ghost as the gift of power upon the sanctified life."[19] Although he did not explicitly define the temporal parameters of "apostolic," he clearly meant the Church described in the New Testament and, in particular, the Church pictured in the Book of Acts. Hence, spiritual life and practice were not only shaped by the Scriptures but needed to be measured by the same Scriptures.

First of all, apostolic holiness meant for Henry a spirituality characterized by a life of disciplined, regular, and intense "prayer and fasting." His diaries show a man who began every day with prayer. He also demanded that his family and anyone visiting their home join him in the same practice. His daughters recall being late for school due to his strictness on this issue.[20] He viewed the prayer of God's people as "vital contact with their Maker."[21] Though prayer certainly meant petitioning God for personal needs, it also included the dimensions of encounter and communion with God. He felt these were particularly important for empowerment in ministry, divine guidance, and personal transformation. Highly respected and acknowledged as a godly man of prayer, Henry visited and prayed for the sick in his local church and the community at large. Invariably, the notation in his diaries for each Friday read "prayed and fasted." Henry faithfully observed the ancient Wesleyan practice of fasting every Friday.

Second, apostolic holiness, in Henry's mind, pointed to a spirituality that relied upon the effective working of the Holy Spirit. Without the definite presence and power of the Holy Spirit, he believed the child of God faced certain failure in life and ministry. He firmly stated with reference to leadership in the church: "This must be on the apostolic order; the Holy Ghost must be the real leader as in the early Church. Otherwise we will make a complete failure." [22]

He constantly pointed to the need for Spirit-filled ministers and young workers. This need demanded a school for education and training. Yet, Henry strongly insisted at the same time that those persons so engaged needed empowerment from on high, needed the Holy Spirit in their souls, and needed "Pentecostal fire." In his own life and for the ministry and responsibility placed in his hands, Henry constantly prayed for "a fresh anointing," "power of the Spirit," and a "mighty outpouring of the Holy Ghost."

Third, Bishop Fisher's understanding of apostolic holiness led him to insist upon a spiritual life and practice that were marked by a willingness to endure personal hardship, sacrifice, and suffering for the sake of spreading the gospel of Jesus Christ. He observed, "The Apostles suffered shame for His name. Their lives were full of sacrifice and self-denial.... They through holy zeal suffered and sacrificed that the gospel would spread through the known world."[23] Consequently, in order to personally carry out what he understood to be his ministry, he freely gave and used his own limited resources. He once returned home from an evangelistic mission of six weeks with 65 cents for his services. His wife, Annie, who voluntarily shared in these rigors of ministry, noted that on his return, all Henry talked about was the many souls that had been saved.[24]

The story of Bishop Fisher's unparalleled accomplishments is incomplete without recognition of Annie Fisher's long hours of toil given to sustain the family and free Henry for ministry. He constantly gave to those in need – to the sick, to orphans, and to widows. During the Great Depression he felt keenly an obligation to help those in greater need. He sent regular support to San Francisco, California, to assist a United Holy Church that was feeding thousands every day. He often borrowed small sums of money in order to take care of his family, travel, and minister for the organization. The image of a soldier in service loomed large in his mind and in the many annual reports he gave over the years. This image was not simply a literary metaphor, but literally described Henry's self-identity and his life of voluntary privation and self-denial for the cause of Jesus Christ.

Bishop Fisher's parents, John Henry and Lucy Fisher, were born into slavery.[25] As a result Henry did not possess the resources to access the full educational opportunities he desired or needed. Yet through his experience of holiness and the empowerment by the Holy Spirit, he tapped into that deep spiritual spring that empowered the early apostles of Jesus Christ and birthed the Wesleyan, Methodist, Holiness, and Pentecostal movements.

Despite the challenges of World War I, the Great Depression, and life in a hostile and racist society, Bishop Henry Lee Fisher's experience of the awesome power of God was a significant and potent factor in causing the United Holy Church of America to grow, expand, and develop during difficult times. His life affected thousands and continues to do so 'til this day. The genius of the spiritual life and practice of H. L. Fisher is simply that he connected with the deep spiritual source that gave and continues to give vitality and power to the Christian Church.

> *The heights of great men reached and kept*
> *were not attained by sudden flight.*
> *But they, while their companions slept,*
> *were toiling in the night.*
> *(Sir Winston Leonard Spenser Churchill)*

UNITED HOLY CHURCH OF AMERICA, INC.

General Presidents:

L. M. Mason
(1894-1901)

W. H. Fulford
(1901-1916)

Henry Lee Fisher
(1916-1947)

G. J. Branch
(1947-1949)

Henry W. Hairston
(1949-1963)

Walter N. Strobhar
(1963-1980)

Joseph T. Bowens
(1980-1992)

Thomas E. Talley
(1992-1996)

Odell McCollum
(1996-2005)

Elijah Williams
(2005 to present)

Author:

Dennis W. Ball

ENDNOTES

Chapter 1
Assemblies of God

1   *Word and Witness.* December 20, 1913, 1. The first paragraph in this essay was adapted with permission from George O. Wood, "Foreword," in Lois Olena, *Stanley M. Horton: Shaper of Pentecostal Theology.* Springfield, MO: Gospel Publishing House, 2009, 7.

2   In 2008, the Assemblies of God (USA) was the largest white and Hispanic Pentecostal denomination in America, with 2.9 million adherents in over 12,300 churches. The Assemblies of God (USA) is a constituent member of the World Assemblies of God Fellowship, which numbered over 61 million believers worldwide.

3   The Church of God in Christ in which Bell served as a leader separated from Charles Parham's Apostolic Faith Movement in 1907. It continued under the name Apostolic Faith Movement until 1910 or 1911, when it changed its name to Church of God in Christ. This largely white group was organizationally distinct from Bishop Charles H. Mason's largely African-American denomination that went by the same name. Informal links between the two groups did exist, and their leaders and members often crossed the color line to worship together. Historians have been unable to locate documentation to show whether a formal connection existed between the two organizations. For more information, see: Darrin Rodgers. "The Assemblies of God and the Long Journey toward Racial Reconciliation," *Assemblies of God Heritage.* 2008, 54-58.

4   The title "General Chairman" was changed to "General Superintendent" in 1927.

5   *Word and Witness.* December 20, 1913, 1.

6   *Word and Witness.* March 20, 1914, 1.

7   [J. Roswell Flower], "Brother E. N. Bell with his Lord." *Pentecostal Evangel.* June 30, 1923, 2.

8   Ethel Goss. *The Winds of God.* Hazelwood, MO: Word Aflame Press, 1958, 245-246.

9   Charles G. Weston republished the tract. He identified the original as Evangel Tract No. 914 published by The Gospel Publishing House, Springfield, MO, between 1914 and 1921. No copy of the original has been found.

10 Ibid., 13.

11 Ibid., 5-6.

12 Some years later he explained his motives for being rebaptized: He wanted to glorify Christ, was uncertain about his original baptism, and never accepted the non-Trinitarian implications of the baptismal formula. E.N. Bell to Pastor J.C. Brickey, August 20, 1920, Flower Pentecostal Heritage Center.

13 "Victory in Failures." *Pentecostal Evangel.* August 26, 1939, 2.

14 E. N. Bell. *Questions and Answers.* Springfield, MO: Gospel Publishing House, 1923, 31.

15 Ibid., 32.

16 Alice Reynolds Flower. *Grace for Grace.* Springfield, MO: n.p., n.d., 58.

17 In 1908 at age 20, J. Roswell began publishing an earlier monthly magazine, *The Pentecost* (later renamed *Grace and Glory*).

18 "The Snare of Sectarianism." *Pentecostal Evangel.* October 23, 1943, 1, 7-9, 12-13.

19 See his notes to General Council Ministers, February 15, 1943; June 12, 1943; and June 17, 1944.

Organizational Statistics
Number of churches (USA): 12,377
Number of constituents (USA): 2,899,701
Number of credentialed ministers (USA): 34,178
Number of students studying for discipleship and leadership: 16,324
Number of countries in which Assemblies of God actively serves: 213
Name of publishing arm: Gospel Publishing House
The Assemblies of God (USA) is a constituent member of the World Assemblies of God Fellowship

(WAGF).

Statistics for WAGF, including the Assemblies of God (USA) are below:
Number of churches: 332, 411
Number of constituents: 61,550,938
Number of ministers: 344,399
Number of students studying for discipleship and leadership: 100,422
* Statistics current as of December 31, 2008

Chapter 2
Association of Vineyard Churches

Organizational Statistics
Number of churches (worldwide): 1,467
Number of churches overseas: 900
Number of constituents: 120,000
Number of credentialed ministers (USA): 603
Number of countries in which Vineyard actively serves: 60
* Statistics current as of October 1, 2009

Chapter 3
Canadian Assemblies of God

1   Ferdinando Zaffuto. Letter sent to Anthony DiGregorio, February 4, 1958. Daniel Ippolito. *History of the Italian Pentecostal Church of Toronto.*
2   Luigi Ippolito. A written testimony of his life and conversion and the beginnings in Hamilton; May 22, 1964.
Daniel Ippolito. *History of the Italian Pentecostal Church of Toronto.* February 29, 1996.
Daniel Ippolito. *History of the Italian Pentecostal Church of Canada.* May, 2002.
3   Ibid., May 22, 1964.
4   Ferdinando Zaffuto. Letter sent to Anthony DiGregorio, February 4, 1958.
5   Felix LiSanti. *History of the Italian Pentecostal Church of Toronto.* Daniel Ippolito, February 29, 1996.
6   Mary Giammatolo. Personal interview with Daniel Ippolito.
7   Mary Croce. Personal interview with Daniel Ippolito.
8   Luigi Guglietti. Letter to Anthony DiGregorio, February 29, 1972.

Organizational Statistics
Number of churches (Canada): 20

Number of constituents: 5,000
Number of credentialed ministers: 70
Number of students studying for discipleship and leadership: 36
Number of countries in which the CAOG actively serves: 5
*Statistics current as of October 10, 2009

Chapter 4
Church of God (Cleveland)

1   R. G. Spurling. *The Lost Link Turtletown,* Tenn.: By author, 1920, 48.
2   Quoted in A.J. Tomlinson's, *The Last Great Conflict.* Cleveland, Tenn.: Press of Walter E. Rodgers, 185-86. Tomlinson's account is the earliest history of the Church of God. The best history of the Spurlings and their ministry is Wade H. Phillips. *A Concise History/Doctrine.* Cleveland, Tenn.: White Wing Publishing House, 1998, 15-19 and Notes.
3   The evangelists were William Martin, Billy Hamby, Joe Tipton and Milton McNabb. Billy Hamby was the brother-in-law of R. G. Spurling, and Milton McNabb was the cousin of W. F. Bryant. Charles W. Conn. *Like a Mighty Army: A History of the Church of God.* 1886-1996, Tribute Edition, Cleveland, Tenn.: Pathway Press, 2008, 24.
4   Quoted in "History of Pentecost." *The Faithful Standard.* September 1922, 6.
5   Quoted in "History of Pentecost." 6. See also Wade H. Phillips, "W. F. Bryant: From Bootlegger to Holiness Leader." *Church of God History and Heritage.* Summer/Fall 2002, 3-5, 13.
6   W. F. Bryant quoted in "Youth Interviews Experience." *The Lighted Pathway.* July 1949, 14. Bryant used language previously published in Tomlinson's, *The Last Great Conflict.* 189. Although Tomlinson is the first to have recorded these events, he would have relied on Bryant's firsthand account.
7   Conn. *Like a Mighty Army.* 31.
8   Bryant quoted in "History of Pentecost." 6.
9   See Liberty Baptist Church, "Minutes," December 1898. Quoted in Wade H. Phillips, "Baptist Rejection of Holiness

Revives the Church of God." *Church of God History and Heritage.* Summer/Fall 2002, 1.

10 Document 8A (Notes from interview with Nettie Bryant and Ella Bryant Robinson) in William F. Bryant File, Dixon Pentecostal Research Center, Cleveland, Tennessee, 2-3; and "History of Pentecost," 20.

11 Quoted in "History of Pentecost." 20.

12 Ibid.

13 R. G. Spurling. "Boy Healed and Baptized with the Holy Ghost – Listen to the Midnight Cry." *Church of God Evangel,* July 15, 1910, 6.

14 Spurling. "Boy Healed and Baptized with the Holy Spirit," 6.

Organizational Statistics:
Number of churches (worldwide): 34,269
Number of constituents (worldwide): 6,945,788
Number of credentialed ministers (worldwide): 45,290
Number of students studying for discipleship and leadership (worldwide): 63,096
Number of countries in which Church of God actively serves: 179
Name of publishing arm: Pathway Press
*Statistics current as of October 2009

Chapter 5
Church of God in Christ
Organizational Statistics
Number of churches: 15,300 (1991)
Number of constituents: Over 6 million (2009)
Number of credentialed ministers: 33,593 (1991)
Number of countries in which Church of Christ actively serves: 56 (1991)
*Statistics taken from the *Yearbook of American & Canadian Churches.* Nashville, TN: Abbington Press, 2009. Current as of 1991.

Chapter 6
Church of God of the Apostolic Faith
1 Grant Wacker uses the terms "primitive" and "pragmatic" to define early

Pentecostals throughout his book *Heaven Below: Early Pentecostals and American Culture.* Cambridge, Mass.: Harvard University Press, 2001.

2 Three brief historical sketches of the COGAF have been written: E.A. Buckles. *A Brief History: The Church of God of the Apostolic Faith.* Drumright, OK: 1935; Gordon J. Melton. *Encyclopedia of American Religions.* 5th ed. Detroit: Gale Research, 1996, 365-366; Arthur Carl Piepkorn. *Profiles in Belief: The Religious Bodies of the United States and Canada.* San Francisco: Harper & Row Publishers, Inc., 1979, 3:121-122. The actual date of the meeting is not known. According to oral history it happened within several months after the April 1914 founding General Council of the Assemblies of God.

3 Richard M. Riss. "Finished Work Controversy" in *The New International Dictionary of Pentecostal and Charismatic Movements,* eds. Stanley M. Burgess and Eduard M. Van Der Maas, Grand Rapids: Zondervan, 2002, 638-639.

4 Vinson Synan. *The Century of the Holy Spirit: 100 Years of Pentecostal and Charismatic Renewal.* Nashville: Thomas Nelson, 2001, 97-122.

5 Charles Ronald French, letter to Wayne and Joyce Taylor, September 16, 2009.

6 E.A. Buckles. *God's Plan of Salvation.* Ozark, AR.: n.d., 11.

7 Ibid.

8 Ibid.

9 Ibid., 10.

10 French, letter.

11 See issues of *The Apostolic Faith Messenger* between 1934 and 1936.

12 E.A. Buckles. *A Brief History: The Church of God of the Apostolic Faith.* Drumright, OK: 1935, 8-9.

13 Ibid., 9-10.

14 Joe L. Edmonson, phone interview by author, October 6, 2009.

15 Buckles. *Brief History.* 18-20.

16 E.A. and E.C. Buckles. "Our Young People." *The Apostolic Faith Messenger.* April 1934.

17 Ibid.

18 Ibid.

19 Joe L. Edmonson, phone interview by author, October 14, 2009.

20 O.H. Bond. *The Life Story of the Rev. O.H.Bond*. Oak Grove, AR.: 1957, 15-26. The book was completed posthumously by his wife, Mrs. Georgia Bond.

21 Ibid., 33.

22 Ibid., 36.

23 Ibid., 38.

24 Ibid., 41.

25 Earnest Buckles. "Brother Bond Called Home." *The Apostolic Faith Messenger*. Jan.-Apr. 1957.

26 Minutes of The COGAF Conference, Mulberry, KS, April 1 and 2, 1919.

27 Minutes of The COGAF Conference, Drumright, OK, December 22, 1924.

28 Buckles. "*Called Home*."

29 "Little paper" was the term used by most, even Bond himself, to refer to the newspaper.

30 O. H. Bond. "The Truth About Pentecost." *The Apostolic Faith Messenger*. Jan.-Feb. 1951.

31 Bond. *Life*. 37.

32 Minutes of The COGAF Conference, Drumright, OK, October 4, 1926.

33 Minutes of The COGAF Conference, Drumright, OK, December 7, 1932.

34 For examples, see *The Apostolic Faith Messenger*, nos. 78 (Feb./Mar. 1940), 96 (Jan./Feb. 1943), and especially 28 (Aug. 1933) where Bond ties the change in standards of dress to the imminent tribulation period.

35 Buckles. "*Called Home*."

36 In 2009 The COGAF reported 53 US congregations with an average Sunday worship attendance of 5,024. The COGAF's Mexican affiliate, Iglesia Cristiana Evangelical Mexicana, claims about 40 congregations.

Organizational Statistics:
Number of churches (worldwide) 93
Number of constituents (U.S.) 5,024
Number of credentialed ministers (U.S.) 136
Number of students studying for discipleship (Merge College): 6.
Number of countries in which COGAF actively serves: 2

Chapter 7
Church of God Mountain Assembly
Organizational Statistics:
Number of churches (worldwide): 615
Number of constituents (worldwide): 46,100
Number of credentialed ministers (worldwide): 605
Number of countries in which Church of God Mountain Assembly actively serves: 24
*Statistics current as of December 17, 2009

Chapter 8
Church of God of Prophecy

1 *Pentecostals from the Inside Out*. Harold B. Smith, Editor, (Christianity Today Series), Victor Books, 1990. See Chapter 9, by Russell P. Spittler, for references to classical Pentecostals.

2 *Azusa Street and Its Legacy*. Harold D. Hunter and Cecil M. Robeck Jr. Editors, Pathway Press, Cleveland, TN, 2006, 117.

3 *The Last Great Conflict*. A. J. Tomlinson, Press of Walter E. Rodgers, 1913; Reprint, White Wing Publishing House and Press, 1984, 233. See also typed copy, Diary of A. J. Tomlinson, CGP Archives, Cleveland, TN, entry for January 13, 1908.

4 Photocopy of Program Outline for 3rd Annual Assembly of the Churches of East Tennessee, North Georgia, Western North Carolina, (on file) Hal Bernard Dixon Jr. Pentecostal Research Center, Cleveland, TN.

5 *The Last Great Conflict:* Reprint, White Wing Publishing House and Press, 1984, 227, 232.

6 Diary of A. J. Tomlinson: Volume III: Homer Tomlinson, Editor, CGP Archives, Cleveland, TN, 13.

7 *The Last Great Conflict*: 232.

8 Ibid., 183.

9 This author remembers growing up in a Pentecostal church in the Virgin Islands where the standard testimony form was "I'm saved, sanctified holy (for some that meant spelling out, 'w-h-o-l-l-y'), filled with the Holy Ghost, and feel like going on." It should be noted that for

many Pentecostals, sanctification as a "second definite work of grace" was not adopted as an intermediate step to Holy Spirit baptism. Even for some classical Pentecostals this is not emphasized as in earlier times although instantaneous sanctification as taught and practiced in some Wesleyan traditions is still among their lists of teachings.

10 *Answering the Call of God – The Marvelous Experiences of A. J. Tomlinson*: White Wing Publishing House, Cleveland TN, 1973, 10-13.

11 Letter of A. J. Tomlinson to his friend Ellis Barker as quoted by Roger G. Robins in *A. J. Tomlinson: Plain Folk Modernist*, Oxford University Press, New York, 2004, 84-85.

12 See typed copy of A. J. Tomlinson's Diary CGP Archives, Cleveland, TN: Diary Entries for October 30, 1897 and October 1, 1901.

13 Diary Entry for May 10th, 1903.

14 *The NEW International Dictionary of Pentecostal and Charismatic Movements (Revised and Expanded Edition)*. Stanley Burgess, Editor and Eduard M Van Der Maas, Associate Editor; Zondervan Publishing House, Grand Rapids, 1143.

15 Ibid., 1144. Hunter's article lists: *Evangelical Visitor, Tongues of Fire, The Mountain Missionary, The Way of Faith, God's Revivalist*, and the *Bible Advocate*.

16 *Book of Minutes. General Assemblies Churches of God*. Church of God Publishing House: Cleveland, TN, 1922, 13.

17 *The Last Great Conflict*. 217.

18 Portions from typed copy of A. J.'s Diary: Entry for October 14, 1908, CGP Archives.

19 C. T. Davidson. *Upon This Rock, Volume I*. White Wing Publishing House and Press, Cleveland, TN, 1973, 604.

20 Ibid. 557-562. See also *Historical Annual Addresses, Volume I*. White Wing Press 1970, 163-167, for A. J. Tomlinson's remarks about the subject under the heading "The Seventy."

21 *Upon This Rock*. 562.

22 *Historical Annual Addresses, Volume I*, 218.

23 Ibid. Note: The more practical, human and organizational issues (power, management, financial problems, and operational style) are not deliberately ignored but space and the specific focus of this writing do not allow for their treatment here. Interested readers are referred to: *Like a Mighty Army (Definitive Edition)* by Charles Conn; *The Holiness Pentecostal Tradition*, by VinsonSynan; *A. J. Tomlinson: Plainfolk Modernist*, by Roger Robins; *The Era of A. J. Tomlinson,* by Daniel Preston and the *Centennial Commemorative Issue* (June, 2003) *White Wing Messenger* – Official publication of the CGP. See especially articles by Vinson Synan and Adrian Varlack.

24 Daniel D. Preston. *The Era of A. J. Tomlinson*. White Wing Publishing House and Press, 1984, 139.

25 *Historical Annual Addresses, Volume I*, 219; The reference to "Church of God" here is to the Church in the biblical sense of the name and to the nature of the Church they originally sought to restore on New Testament lines before the Assembly added what they now considered extra-biblical structures.

26 *Historical Annual Addresses Volume I*. 219-220.

27 Davidson. *Upon This Rock* – 368, gives the dates each of the other family members received the baptism as follows: Halcy Olive (a daughter) August 10, 1908; Homer Aubry (son) August 18, 1908; Mary Jane (wife to A. J. Tomlinson) August 21, 1908; Iris Marea (a daughter) July 23, 1909; Milton Ambrose (son) August 14, 1927.

28 See 1952 Minutes of the 47th Assembly, The Church of God of Prophecy, 28-30 for the explanation by M. A. Tomlinson who succeeded his father as General Overseer in 1943.

29 For additional treatment of A. J. Tomlinson and other founders whose Spirit-led influences affected both groups, see the chapter (in this volume) on The Church of God, Cleveland, Tennessee, by Dr. David Roebuck.

Organizational Statistics:

Number of churches (worldwide): 9,295
Number of constituents: 1,334,672
Number of credentialed ministers
(worldwide): 9,400
Number of students studying for
discipleship and leadership: 8,634
Number of countries in which Church
of God of Prophecy actively serves: 127
Name of publishing arm: White Wing
Publishing House
*Statistics current as of August 31, 2008

Chapter 9
Elim Fellowship

1   Marion Meloon. *Ivan Spencer: Willow
    in the Wind.*
2   Ivan Q. Spencer. *Faith: Living the
    Crucified Life.* Furrow Press, www.
    furrowpress.com.
3   *Ivan Q. Spencer. Daily Seedings: A
    Devotional Classic for the Spirit-filled
    Life* (Furrow Press (www.furrowpress.
    com). All quoted materials were used
    with permission.

Organizational Statistics:
Number of churches (U.S.): 86
Number of credentialed ministers (U.S.):
713
Number of students studying for
discipleship and leadership (U.S.): 160
Number of countries in which Elim
Fellowship actively ministers: 26
*Statistics are current as of November
22, 2009

Chapter 10
Full Gospel Fellowship of
Churches and Ministers, Int'l.

1   Gordon Lindsay, *The Gordon Lindsay
    Story.* Texas: Christ For The Nations,
    Inc. 1992, 1.
2   Ibid., 66.
3   Ibid., 127.
4   Ibid., 142.
5   Ibid., 145.
6   Ibid., 157.
7   Ibid., 191-200.

Organizational Statistics:
Churches (worldwide): 698 worldwide
Ministerial Organizations (worldwide):
590

Number of constituents (worldwide):
105,905
Number of credentialed ministers
(worldwide): 881
Number of countries in which The
Fellowship actively serves: 35
*Statistics current as of October 29,
2009

Chapter 11
Independent Assemblies of God
International (Canada)
Source:
J. R. Colletti. "Rasmussen, Andrew W."
*Dictionary of Pentecostal and
Charismatic Movements.* 1988.

Organizational Statistics:
Number of churches (worldwide): 570
Number of credentialed ministers
(worldwide): 711
*Statistics are current as of September 1,
2009

Chapter 12
International Church of the
Foursquare Gospel
Sources:
International Church of the Foursquare
Gospel: "Our Founder," www.
foursquare.org/ landing_pages/8, 3.
Aimee Semple McPherson. 1923,
(reprint 1996). *This is That.* Los Angeles:
Foursquare Publications. (Note: This
book provided the basis for much of
the content that was condensed in this
chapter; specific pages are referenced as
necessary.)
Nathaniel M. Van Cleave, 1994. *The
Vine and the Branches: A History of the
International Church of the Foursquare
Gospel.* Los Angeles: Foursquare
Publications. (Note: This book provided
some of the information that was
condensed for this chapter; no specific
pages are referenced.)

Organizational Statistics:
Number of churches (worldwide):
59,620
Number of constituents (worldwide):
8,439,618

Number of credentialed ministers
(worldwide): 70,029
Number of countries in which
Foursquare actively serves: 142
Name of publishing arm: Foursquare
Media
*Statistics current as of December 31,
2008

Chapter 13
International Pentecostal Church of Christ

Attribution: Most of the above material has been gleaned from the notes of Dr. Chester I. Miller, Archivist for the International Pentecostal Church of Christ (1954-2003).

Organizational Statistics:
Number of churches (worldwide): 539
(approximate and associated)
Number of constituents: 4,807
Number of credentialed ministers in the USA: 147
Number of countries in which IPCC actively serves: 12
Name of publishing arm: The Pentecostal Leader
*Statistics current as of March 31, 2009

Chapter 14
International Pentecostal Holiness Church

Sources:
Doug Beacham. *Azusa East: The Life and Times of G.B. Cashwell.* Franklin Springs, GA: LifeSprings Resources, 2006.
Stanley Burgess. *The New International Dictionary of Pentecostal Charismatic Movements.* Grand Rapids, MI: Zondervan, 2002, 2003.
Cecil M. Robeck, Jr. *The Azusa Street Mission and Revival.* Nashville, TN: Thomas Nelson, Inc., 2006.
Vinson Synan. *The Old Time Power: A Centennial History of the International Pentecostal Holiness Church.* Franklin Springs, GA: LifeSprings Resources, 1998.
Organizational Statistics:
Number of churches (worldwide):

17,883
Number of constituents (worldwide):
4,175,481
Number of credentialed ministers
(worldwide): 22,500
Number of students studying for
discipleship and leadership (worldwide):
6,000
Number of countries in which IPHC
actively serves: 103
Name of publishing arm: LifeSprings
Resources
*Statistics current as of January 1, 2009

Chapter 15
Open Bible Churches

Sources:
R. Bryant Mitchell. *Heritage & Horizons.* Open Bible Standard Publishers, 1982. The *Open Bible Messenger* and *Message of the Open Bible* (Open Bible Standard Publishers).
Fred Hornshuh, Sr. *Big Game Hunting*
Fred Hornshuh, Sr. *Nuggets and Cogitations of a 95-Year-Old Preacher.*
Fred Hornshuh, Sr., *Historical Sketches of the Bible Standard Churches.*

Organizational Statistics:
Number of churches (worldwide): 1,700
Number of constituents (worldwide):
160,000
Number of credentialed ministers
(worldwide): 3,100
Number of students studying for
discipleship and leadership (worldwide):
10,000**
Number of countries in which Open
Bible Churches actively serves: 45
Name of publishing arm: OBC
Publishing
*Statistics current as of June 2009.
** Many students enrolled in INSTE
from other denominations are included
in this number.

Chapter 16
Open Bible Faith Fellowship of Canada

1   Pearl D. Griffith. *Relay of Our Faith.*
    Trinadad: P.D.G. Publishing, 2004,
    55–59.

Additional Sources:
Interview by Dr. Don Bryan with Harry Armoogan, January 15, 2010.
Interview by Dr. Don Bryan with Harry Armoogan, February 1, 2010.
Open Bible archives, file, Armond O. Ramseyer.

Organizational Statistics:
Number of churches (worldwide): 152
Number of constituents (worldwide): 7,000
Number of credentialed ministers (worldwide): 477
Number of students studying for discipleship and leadership: Approx. 1,500
Number of countries in which OBFF actively serves: 10
*Statistics current as of October 2009

Chapter 17
Pentecostal Assemblies of Canada, The

1　Carl Brumback. *Suddenly ... from heaven.* Springfield, MO: Gospel Publishing, 1961, 48, 62-63.
2　Charles F. Parham. *The Apostolic Faith.* September 1906, 1.
3　Bennett F. Lawrence, *The Apostolic Faith Restored.* Springfield, MO: Gospel Publishing, 1916, 12.
4　Ellen Hebden. "How Pentecost Came to Toronto." *The Promise*, 1 (May 1907); see also William Seymour. *The Apostolic Faith, 1:6* (February-March 1907): 4.
5　Ellen Hebden. *The Promise.* 15 (March 1910): 1.
6　Ibid.
7　Thomas William Miller. *Canadian Pentecostals: A History of The Pentecostal Assemblies of Canada.* Edited by William A. Griffin, Mississauga, ON: Full Gospel Publishing House, 1994, 44; see also Miller. "The Canadian 'Azusa': The Hebden Mission in Toronto." *Pneuma*, 8:1 (Spring 1986), 5-29.
8　Abridged passages about McAlister and Argue are taken with permission from Miller's *Canadian Pentecostals*.
9　*The Doctrine and Discipline of the Holiness Movement.* Ottawa, ON:

Holines Movement Publishing House, 1907.
10　*The Promise.* 15, March 1910, 1.
11　Recorded interview with G. F. Atter, April 30, 1984.
12　G. F. Atter. *The Third Force.* Peterborough, ON: College Press, 3rd ed. rev. (1962), 74.
13　A. H. Argue. "Azusa Street Revival Reaches Winnipeg." *The Pentecostal Testimony.* May 1956: 9.
14　A. G. Ward. "How the Pentecostal Experience Came to Canada." Typed copy, PAOC Archives.
15　His interest in divine healing led Argue to establish a close connection with Mrs. Woodworth-Etter, the famous healing evangelist. He shared in the dedication service for her new tabernacle in Indianapolis, and then assisted her at the 1913 World-Wide Camp Meeting at Los Angeles.
16　Thomas Miller. "The Significance of A. H. Argue for Pentecostal Historiography," *Pneuma*, 8:2 (Fall 1986): 120-158.
17　*The Apostolic Faith.* 2:13, May 1908: 4.
18　Recorded interview with Walter E. McAlister, May 3, 1984.

Organizational Statistics:
Number of churches (Canada): 1,104
Number of constituents (Canada): 233,400
Number of credentialed ministers (Canada): 3,551
Number of students studying for discipleship and leadership (worldwide): 18,706**
Number of countries in which PAOC actively serves: 52
*Statistics current as of January 5, 2009
**Statistics on discipleship and online courses in Canada are unavailable

Chapter 18
Pentecostal Assemblies of Newfoundland and Labrador

1　I am grateful to Cathy Anstey, George Dawe, and David Newman for reading this chapter and making several valuable suggestions.
2　On Alice Belle Garrigus, see her

"Walking In the King's Highway." *Good Tidings*. September 1938-December 1942; also available at http://www.mun.ca/rels/pent/texts/king.html (accessed March 25, 2008).
In addition, see Burton K. Janes. *The Lady Who Came: The Biography of Alice Belle Garrigus, Newfoundland's First Pentecostal Pioneer*, vol. 1 (1858-1908). St. John's, *Newfoundland*: Good Tidings Press, 1982;
The Lady Who Stayed: The Biography of Alice Belle Garrigus, Newfoundland's First Pentecostal Pioneer, vol. 2 (1908-1949). St. John's, *Newfoundland*: Good Tidings Press, 1983;
History of the Pentecostal Assemblies of Newfoundland. St. John's, Newfoundland: Good Tidings Press, 1996, especially Chapters 1-2;
"Alice Belle Garrigus: Newfoundland's First Pentecostal Pioneer," *World Pentecost* (XII:3), 8-10;
"Walking in the King's Highway: Alice Belle Garrigus and the Pentecostal Movement in Newfoundland," *Assemblies of God Heritage* (VI:2), Summer 1986, 3f., 14;
"Alice Belle Garrigus," Joseph R. Smallwood, ed.-in-chief, *Encyclopedia of Newfoundland and Labrador*, vol. 2, St. John's, Newfoundland: Newfoundland Book Publishers [1967] Ltd., 1984, pp. 485f.;
James A. Hewett, "Alice Belle Garrigus," Stanley M. Burgess, ed., *The New International Dictionary of Pentecostal and Charismatic Movements*, rev. ed. Grand Rapids, Michigan: Zondervan, 2002, 661;
Hans Rollmann, "From Yankee Failure to Newfie Success: The Indigenization of the Pentecostal Movement in Newfoundland," Hans Rollmann, *Religious Studies 3901 – Religion in Newfoundland and Labrador: The Nineteenth and Twentieth Centuries*, St. John's, Newfoundland: Memorial University of Newfoundland Printing Services, second ed 1990 [1988], 6.33-6.41;
Joseph R. Smallwood. "Alice B. Garrigus," Joseph R. Smallwood, ed., *The Book of Newfoundland*, vol. 5, St. John's, Newfoundland: Newfoundland Book Publishers [1967] Ltd., 1975, 568. The most up-to-date research on Garrigus currently available is found in Kurt O. Berends' thesis, "A Divided Harvest: Alice Belle Garrigus, Joel Adams Wright, and Early New England Pentecostalism." Wheaton College Graduate School, 1993.

3   Alice B. Garrigus. "Walking." Good *Tidings*. September 1938, 9.
4   Ibid., 12.
5   Berends."A Divided Harvest," 10.
6   Garrigus. "Walking." Good Tidings. September 1938, 12.
7   Hannah W. Smith. *The Christian's Secret of a Happy Life*. Old Tappan, New Jersey: Fleming H. Revell Company, reprinted 1952 [1875].
8   Garrigus."Walking." *Good Tidings*. March 1939, 17.
9   Ibid., 18.
10 Loc. cit.
11 Loc. cit.
12 Garrigus. "Walking." *Good Tidings*. June 1939, 2.
13 Muriel Wright Evans and Elizabeth M. Evans. *Incidents and Information of the First 48 Years Rumney Conferences 75th Anniversary*. Rumney, New Hampshire: New England Fellowship of Evangelicals, 1978, 1.
14 Berends. "A Divided Harvest." 31.
15 Garrigus. "Walking." *Good Tidings*. September 1939, 10.
16 Ibid., 11.
17 Loc. cit.
18 Loc. cit.
19 Garrigus. "Walking." *Good Tidings*. March 1940, 9. Emphasis in original.
20 Garrigus. "Walking." *Good Tidings*. September 1940, 6.
21 Hewett. "Alice Belle Garrigus." Burgess, ed., *The New International Dictionary of Pentecostal and Charismatic Movements*. 661.
22 Joseph R. Smallwood. *I Chose Canada*. Toronto, Ontario: The Macmillan

Company of Canada Limited, 1973, 89.

Organizational Statistics
Number of churches (Newfoundland
and Canada): 124
Number of constituents: 24,670
Number of credentialed ministers
(2006/2007): 415
Number of countries in which PAONL
actively serves: Works in cooperation
with Pentecostal Assemblies of Canada
in coordinating international missions.
*Statistics current as of 2005

Chapter 19
Pentecostal Church of God
1   Grant Wacker. *Heaven Below: Early
    Pentecostals and American Culture.*
    Harvard University Press, 264.
2   Larry Martin. *We've Come This Far
    by Faith.* Pensacola, FL: Christian Life
    Books, 2009, 19.
3   Martin. 19.
4   *The Pentecostal Herald.* October 1919, 3.
5   *The Pentecostal Herald.* August 1919, 1.
6   *he Pentecostal Herald.* October 1919, 2.
7   Eli DePriest. *The Story of My Life.*
    Self published, printed by Messenger
    Publishing House, 32.
8   Larry Martin. *We've Come This Far by
    Faith.* 40.
9   LaPorte County, Indiana Records,
    Certificate of Death, John C. Sinclair.
10 E. N. Bell to J. Narver Gortner, March
    26, 1923, Flower Pentecostal Heritage
    Center.
11 "John Chalmers Sinclair." *LaPorte
    Herald.* February 28, 1936.
12 *The Pentecostal Messenger.* Vol. 7,
    Number 10, September 15, 1934.
13 Aaron Wilson. *Our Story.* Messenger
    Publishing House, 88.
14 Wilson. 116.
15 Wilson. 113.
16 Wilson. 111.
17 Wilson. 94.

Organizational Statistics:
Number of churches (worldwide): 4,825
Number of constituents (worldwide):
620,000
Number of credentialed ministers
(worldwide): 6,750

Number of countries in which
Pentecostal Church of God actively
serves: 60

Chapter 20
Pentecostal Free Will Baptist
Organizational Statistics
Number of churches (worldwide): 451
Number of constituents (worldwide):
36,401
Number of credentialed ministers
(worldwide): 653
Number of students for discipleship and
leadership (worldwide): 171
Number of countries in which
Pentecostal Free Will Baptist actively
serves: 16
*Statistics current as of October 20,
2009

Chapter 21
**Pentecostal Holiness
Church of Canada**
Sources:
IPHC Web site: iphc.org
A fuller treatment of Bishop King by
Dr. David Alexander was published in
Pneuma: *The Journal of the Society for
Pentecostal Studies* (Fall 1986) under
the title "Bishop J.H. King and the
Emergence of Holiness Pentecostalism."

Organizational Statistics:
Number of churches (Canada): 38
Number of constituents (Canada): 3,000

Chapter 22
**United Holy Church of
America, Inc.**
1   H. L. Fisher. *History of the United Holy
    Church of America, Inc.* n.p., n.d., p. 14.
2   Vinson Synan. The *Holiness-Pentecostal
    Tradition.* Grand Rapids: Eerdmans,
    1997, 22-83.
3   Fisher. *History.* 5.
4   Fisher. Personal Diary, November 24,
    1922.
5   U.S. Bureau of the Census, 1880 United
    States Census Household Record,
    http:// www.familysearch.org/Eng/
    Search/ census/household record
    [accessed May 21, 2003].
6   Fisher. *History.* 10.
7   Official Journal, The United Holy

Church of America, 24th Annual Convocation (Winston-Salem, NC: n.p., September 1-8, 1918) 20. The register of churches was limited by the ability of local congregations to send the pastor or delegate to the annual meeting and whether a chosen representative did not attend for some other excusable reason. The number of churches listed would not reflect the exact total, but comparatively reflects growth and participation ofchurches in the life of the organization.

8   1948 Yearbook of the United Holy Church of America (Incorporated)

9   Fisher. *History*. 8-9.

10 *The Works of John Wesley.* Vol. 8, Grand Rapids: Baker Books, 1872, 300. Reprint.

11 1918 Yearbook. 11.

12 Fisher. *History*. 11.

13 Ibid., 24.

14 Ibid., 15.

15 1918 Yearbook. 15.

16 1918 Yearbook. 19.

17 Fisher. 1910 Manual, 3.

18 Fisher. 1910 Manual, 3.

19 Fisher. 1917 Manual, 13.

20 Interview with Grace Medlin Fisher, 2003; interview with Lillian Fisher Amis, 2003.

21 Andrew William Lawson. *The Life of Henry Lee Fisher*. BD thesis, Shaw University School of Divinity, Raleigh, North Carolina, 1948, 19-20.

22 1921 Yearbook. 14.

23 1940 Yearbook. 9.

24 Lawson. *History*. 9.

25 Ibid., 1.

Organizational Statistics:
Number of churches (worldwide): 800
Number of credentialed ministers (worldwide): 1,931
Number of countries in which United Holy Church of America, Inc. actively serves: 12
*Statistics current as of November 3, 2009

MEMPHIS 1994:
MIRACLE & MANDATE

By Dr. Vinson Synan

It was a day never to be forgotten in the annals of American Pentecostalism, October 18, 1994, when the Spirit moved in Memphis to end decades of racial separation and open doors to a new era of cooperation and fellowship between African-American and white Pentecostals. At the time, it was called the "Memphis Miracle" by those gathered in Memphis as well as in the national press, which hailed the historic importance of the event.

It was called a miracle because it ended decades of formal separation between the predominantly black and white Pentecostal churches in America. In its beginnings, the Pentecostal movement inherited the interracial ethos of the Holiness Movement at the turn of the century. One of the miracles of the Azusa Street revival was the testimony that "the color line was washed away in the Blood." Here in the worldwide cradle of the movement a black man, William J. Seymour, served as pastor of a small black church in Los Angeles, where from 1906 to 1909, thousands of people of all races gathered to received the baptism in the Holy Spirit with the accompanying evidence of speaking in tongues. Often black hands were laid upon white heads to pray down the power of Pentecost. From Azusa Street the movement spread to the nations and continents of the world.

In the beginning, practically all the Pentecostal movements and churches in America were inter-racial, with many having thriving black leaders and churches. But from 1908 to 1924, one by one, most churches bowed to the American system of segregation by separating into racially-segregated fellowships. In "Jim Crow" America, segregation in all areas of life ruled the day. Gradually Seymour's Azusa Street dream of openness and equality faded into historical memory.

The PFNA

The separation of black and white Pentecostals was formalized in 1948 with the creation of the all-white Pentecostal Fellowship of North America (PFNA) in Des Moines, Iowa. As incredible as it seems today, no black churches were invited. The races continued to drift further and further apart.

But by the 1990s the climate had changed drastically in the United States. The civil rights movements and legislation of the 1950s and '60s swept away the last vestiges of legal "Jim Crow" segregation in American life. Schools were integrated. Many doors were opened for all to enter into American public life. Most churches, however, remained segregated and out of touch with these currents. The year 1948 also saw the beginnings of the salvation-healing crusades of Oral Roberts and other Pentecostal evangelists. Both blacks and whites flocked together to the big tent services. Along with Billy Graham, Oral Roberts and other Pentecostal evangelists refused to seat the races in separate areas. Although the churches remained separate, there was more interracial worship among blacks and whites who flocked together to the big tent services.

The advent of the charismatic movement in 1960 and the creation of the Society for Pentecostal Studies (SPS) in 1970 brought more contacts between black and white Pentecostals. The congresses sponsored by the North American Renewal Service Committee (NARSC) in the 1980s and 1990s also brought many black and white Pentecostal leaders together for the first time while serving on the Steering Committee to plan the massive charismatic rallies in New Orleans, Indianapolis, and Orlando.

The Architects Of Unity

The leaders, who above all, brought the races together in Memphis in 1994 were Bishop Ithiel Clemmons of the Church of God in Christ (COGIC), and Bishop Bernard E. Underwood of the International Pentecostal Holiness Church. These men had met while serving on the NARSC board planning the New Orleans Congress of 1987. With great trust and mutual dedication, these two men were able to lay the groundwork for the 1994 meeting in Memphis.

The process began when Underwood was elected to head the PFNA in 1991. At that time he purposed in his heart to use his term to end the racial divide between the Pentecostal churches. On March 6, 1992, the Board of Administration voted unanimously to "pursue the possibility of reconciliation with our African-American brethren." After this, there were four important meetings on the road to Memphis.

The first meeting was on July 31, 1992, in Dallas, Texas, in the DFW Hyatt Regency Hotel where COGIC Bishop O. T. Jones captivated the PFNA leaders with his wit and wisdom. The second meeting was held in Phoenix, Arizona, on January 4-5, 1993, where COGIC pastor Reuben Anderson from Compton, California (representing Bishop Charles Blake) played a key role in bringing understanding of the challenges of urban ministries in America. The third session convened at the PFNA annual meeting in Atlanta, Georgia, on October 25-27, 1993. Here, Jack Hayford of the International Church of the Foursquare Gospel and Bishop Gilbert Patterson, of the Church of God in Christ, strongly affirmed the plans for reconciliation. A fourth meeting in Memphis in January 1994 became known as the "20/20 Meeting" because 20 whites and 20 blacks joined to plan the climactic conference that was planned for October 1994 in Memphis. There, it was hoped, the old PFNA could be laid to rest in order to birth a new fellowship without racial or ethnic boundaries.

The Memphis Miracle

When the delegates arrived in Memphis on October 17, 1994, there was an electric air of expectation that something wonderful was about to happen. The conference theme was "Pentecostal Partners: A Reconciliation Strategy for 21st Century Ministry." Over 3,000 persons attended the evening sessions in the Dixon-Meyers Hall of the Cook Convention Center in downtown Memphis. Everyone was aware of the racial strife in Memphis where Martin Luther King, Jr. was assassinated in 1968. Here, it was hoped, a great racial healing would take place. The night services reflected the tremendous work done by the local committee in the months before the gathering. Bishop Gilbert Patterson of the Temple of Deliverance Church of God in Christ, and Samuel Middlebrook, Pastor of the Raleigh Assembly of God in Memphis, co-chaired the committee. Although both men had pastored in the same city for 29 years, they had never met. The Memphis project brought them together.

The morning sessions were remarkable for the honesty and candor of the papers that were presented by a team of leading Pentecostal scholars. These included Dr. Cecil M. Robeck, Jr. of Fuller Theological Seminary and the Assemblies of God, Dr. Leonard Lovett of the Church of God in Christ, Dr. William Turner of Duke University and the United Holy Church, and Dr. Vinson Synan of Regent University and the Pentecostal Holiness Church. In these sessions, the sad history of separation, racism and neglect was laid bare before the 1,000 or more leaders assembled. These sometimes chilling confessions brought a stark sense of past injustice and the absolute need of repentance and reconciliation. The evening worship sessions were full of Pentecostal fire and fervor as Bishop Patterson, Billy Joe Daugherty, and Jack Hayford preached rousing sermons to the receptive crowds.

The climactic moment, however, came in the scholar's session on the afternoon of October 18, after Bishop Blake tearfully told the delegates, "Brothers and Sisters, I commit my love to you. There are problems down the road, but a strong commitment to love will overcome them all."

Suddenly there was a sweeping move of the Holy Spirit over the entire assembly. A young, black brother uttered a spirited message in tongues after which Jack Hayford hurried to the microphone to give the interpretation. He began by saying, "For the Lord would speak to you this day, by the tongue, by the quickening of the Spirit, and He would say":

> *My sons and my daughters, look, if you will, from the heavenward side of things, and see where you have been, two, separate streams, that is, streams as at floodtide. For I have poured out of my Spirit upon you and flooded you with grace in both your circles of gathering and fellowship. But as streams at floodtide, nonetheless, the waters have been muddied to some degree. Those of desperate thirst have come, nonetheless, for muddy water is better than none at all.*
>
> *My sons and my daughters, if you will look and see that there are some not come to drink because of what they have seen. You have not been aware of it, for only heaven has seen those who would doubt what flowed in your midst, because of the waters muddied having been soiled by the clay of your humanness, not by your crudity, lucidity, or intentionality, but by the clay of your humanness the river has been made impure.*
>
> *But look. Look, for I, by My Spirit, am flowing the two streams into one. And the two becoming one, if you can see from the heaven side of things, are being purified and not only is there a new purity coming in your midst, but there will be multitudes more who will gather at this one mighty river because they will*

see the purity of the reality of My love manifest in you. And so, know that as heaven observes and tells us what is taking place, there is reason for you to rejoice and prepare yourself for here shall be multitudes more than ever before come to this joint surging of my grace among you, says the Lord.

Immediately, a white pastor appeared in the wings of the backstage with a towel and basin of water. His name was Donald Evans, an Assemblies of God pastor from Tampa, Florida. When he explained that the Lord had called him to wash the feet of a black leader as a sign of repentance, he was given access to the platform. In a moment of tearful contrition, he washed the feet of Bishop Clemmons while begging forgiveness for the sins of the whites against their black brothers and sisters. A wave of weeping swept over the auditorium. Then, Bishop Blake approached Thomas Trask, General Superintendent of the Assemblies of God, and tearfully washed his feet as a sign of repentance for any animosity blacks had harbored against their white brothers and sisters. This was the climactic moment of the conference. Everyone sensed that this was the final seal of Holy Spirit approval from the heart of God over the proceedings. In an emotional speech the next day, Dr. Paul Walker of the Church of God (Cleveland, TN) called this event, "the Miracle in Memphis," a name that struck and made headlines around the world.

That afternoon, the members of the old PFNA gathered for the final session of its history. In a very short session, a motion was carried to dissolve the old, all-white organization in favor of a new entity that would be birthed the next day. But more reconciliation was yet to come!

When the new constitution was read to the delegates on October 19, a new name was proposed for the group – Pentecostal Churches of North America (PCNA). It was suggested that the governing board of the new group have equal numbers of blacks and whites and that denominational charter memberships would be welcomed that very day. But before the constitution came before the assembly for a vote, Pastor Billy Joe Daugherty of Tulsa's Victory Christian Center asked the delegates to include the word "charismatic" in the new name. Over a hastily-called luncheon meeting of the "Restructuring Committee," it was agreed that those Christians who thought of themselves as "Charismatics" would also be invited to join. When the vote was taken, the body unanimously voted to call the new organization the Pentecostal and Charismatic Churches of North America (PCCNA). Thus the Memphis Miracle included the beginning of healing between Pentecostals and Charismatics as well as between blacks and whites.

Another milestone of the day was the unanimous adoption of a "Racial Reconciliation Manifesto" that was drafted by Bishop Ithiel Clemmons, Dr. Cecil M. Robeck, Jr., Dr. Leonard Lovett, and Dr. Harold D. Hunter. In this historic document, the new PCCNA pledged to "oppose racism prophetically in all its various manifestations" and to be "vigilant in the struggle." They further agreed to "confess that racism is a sin and as a blight must be condemned" – while promising to "seek partnerships and exchange pulpits with persons of a different hue – in the spirit of our Blessed Lord who prayed that we might be one."

After this, the election of officers took place with Bishop Clemmons chosen as Chairman and Bishop Underwood as Vice-Chairman. Also elected to the Board was Bishop Barbara Amos, whose election demonstrated the resolve of the new organization to bridge the gender gap as well. The other officers represented a balance of blacks and whites from the constituent membership.

The Memphis Mandate

The subsequent meetings of the PCCNA in Memphis in 1996 and Washington, D.C., in 1997 have shown that the road to racial reconciliation in America will not be short or easy. Everyone agrees that there is much more to be done and much to overcome.

The incredible "Memphis Miracle" has now become the "Memphis Mandate." All Spirit-filled believers must join in a crusade of love and goodwill to show the world that when the Spirit moves, those who have been baptized in the Holy Spirit will move forward to bring the lost to Christ, and to full ministry and fellowship, in churches that have no racial, ethnic or gender barriers.

Dr. Vinson Synan, Dean Emeritus of Regent University School of Divinity, has served as an advisor to the PCCNA Executive Committee. Author of the widely-read Holiness-Pentecostal Tradition *and* The Century of the Holy Spirit, *Dr. Synan served as chair of the North American Renewal Service Committee (NARSC) and is an ordained minister with the International Pentecostal Holiness Church.*

MEMPHIS, TENNESSEE
OCTOBER 17-19, 1994

RACIAL RECONCILIATION MANIFESTO

Challenged by the reality of our racial divisions, we have been drawn by the Holy Spirit to Memphis, Tennessee, October 17-19, 1994, in order to become true "Pentecostal Partners" and to develop together "A Reconciliation Strategy for 21st Century Ministry." We desire to covenant together in the ongoing task of racial reconciliation by committing ourselves to the following agenda.

I.   I pledge in concert with my brothers and sisters of many hues to oppose racism prophetically in all its various manifestations within and without the Body of Christ and to be vigilant in the struggle with all my God-given might.

II. I am committed personally to treat those in the Fellowship* who are not of my race or ethnicity, regardless of color, with love and respect as my sisters and brothers in Christ. I am further committed to work against all forms of personal and institutional racism, including those which are revealed within the very structures of our environment.

III. With complete bold and courageous honesty, we mutually confess that racism is sin and as a blight in the Fellowship must be condemned for having hindered the maturation of spiritual development and mutual sharing among Pentecostal-Charismatic believers for decades.

IV. We openly confess our shortcomings and our participation in the sin of racism by our silence, denial, and blindness. We admit the harm it has brought to generations born and unborn. We strongly contend that the past does not always completely determine the future. New horizons are emerging. God wants to do a new thing through His people.

V. We admit that there is no single solution to racism in the Fellowship. We pray and are open to tough love and radical repentance with deep sensitivity to the Holy Spirit as Liberator.

VI. Together we will work to affirm one another's strengths and acknowledge our own weaknesses and inadequacies, recognizing that all of us only "see in a mirror dimly" what God desires to do in this world. Together, we affirm the wholeness of the Body of Christ as fully inclusive of Christians regardless of color. We, therefore, commit ourselves "to love one another with mutual affection, outdoing one another in showing honor (Romans 12:10)."

VII. We commit ourselves not only to pray but also to work for genuine and visible manifestations of Christian unity.

VIII. We hereby commit ourselves not only to the task of making prophetic denouncement of racism in word and creed, but to live by acting in deed. We will fully support and encourage those among us who are attempting change.

IX. We pledge that we will return to our various constituencies and appeal to them for logistical support and intervention as necessary in opposing racism. We will seek partnerships and exchange pulpits with persons of a different hue, not in a paternalistic sense, but in the Spirit of our Blessed Lord who prayed that we might be one (John 17:21).

X. We commit ourselves to leaving our comfort zones, lay aside our warring, racial allegiances, respecting the full humanity of all, live with an openness to authentic liberation, which is a product of Divine Creation, until the shackles fall and all bondage ceases.

XI. At the beginning of the twentieth century, the Azusa Street Mission was a model of preaching and living the Gospel message in the world. We desire to drink deeply from the well of Pentecost as it was embodied in that mission. We, therefore, pledge our commitment to embrace the essential commitments of that mission in evangelism and mission, in justice and holiness, in spiritual renewal and empowerment, and in the reconciliation of all Christians regardless of race or gender as we move into the new millennium.

Manifesto Committee:
> **Ithiel Clemmons**
> **Leonard Lovett**
> **Cecil M. Robeck, Jr.**
> **Harold D. Hunter**

*"Fellowship" refers to the PFNA (Pentecostal Fellowship of North America).

CONSTITUTION PREAMBLE

At the beginning of the twentieth century, the Pentecostal movement was born in America out of several Holiness and deeper-life movements. The identifying teaching of the Pentecostal movement centered on the experience known as the baptism in the Holy Spirit, evidenced by speaking in tongues and other gifts of the Spirit. Beginning in Topeka, Kansas, in 1901, the movement became a worldwide force after 1906, through the Azusa Street Mission in Los Angeles, California. From a small group led by African Americans, the movement soon became interracial and international, encompassing people of all races, cultures, denominations, and nationalities.

The purpose of the Pentecostal/Charismatic Churches of North America is to provide a framework for fellowship, dialogue, and cooperation between the various Pentecostal and Charismatic denominations, churches, and ministries in North America that agree with the purposes and goals of the organization. Since these churches and fellowships share a common history of Holy Spirit renewal and an overriding goal of evangelizing the world, they wish to join in a common witness to the outpouring of the Holy Spirit upon all flesh in the last days.

It is the desire of the Pentecostal/Charismatic Churches of North America to give expression to the inherent principles of spiritual unity and fellowship among Pentecostal believers, leaving inviolate the existing forms of government adopted by its members and recognizing that every freedom and privilege enjoyed by any group shall remain its undisturbed possession.

The Pentecostal/Charismatic Churches of North America are committed to the message of reconciliation through the cross and unity in the power of the Holy Spirit, which became a reality on the Day of Pentecost and was demonstrated at the outpouring of the Holy Spirit at Azusa Street at the beginning of the twentieth century.

PCCNA Chairpersons

1994 – 1997
Ithiel Clemmons, Chairperson
Bernard Underwood, Co-Chairperson

1997 – 1999
Thomas Trask, Co-Chairperson
Gilbert Patterson, Co-Chairperson

1999 – 2001
Barbara Amos, Co-Chairperson
Billy Joe Daugherty, Co-Chairperson

2001 – 2005
James Leggett, Co-Chairperson
George McKinney, Co-Chairperson

2005 – 2006
Charles Crabtree, Chairperson
Jerry Macklin, Co-Chairperson

2006 – 2009
Jerry Macklin, Chairperson
William Morrow, Co-Chairperson

2009 – Present
Jeff Farmer, Chairperson
Jerry Macklin, Co-Chairperson

Member Organizations
of the PCCNA
2009

Assemblies of God
Association of Vineyard Churches
Canadian Assemblies of God
Church of God
Church of God in Christ
Church of God of the Apostolic Faith
Church of God Mountain Assembly
Church of God of Prophecy
Congregational Holiness Church
Elim Fellowship
The Foursquare Church
Full Gospel Fellowship
Independent Assemblies of God Int'l
Independent Assemblies of God Int'l (Canada)
International Center for Spiritual Renewal
Int'l Fellowship of Christian Assemblies
Int'l Pentecostal Church of Christ
Int'l Pentecostal Holiness Church
Open Bible Churches
Open Bible Faith Fellowship
Pentecostal Assemblies of Canada
Pentecostal Assemblies of Newfoundland
Pentecostal Church of God
Pentecostal Free Will Baptist Church
Pentecostal Holiness Church of Canada
United Evangelical Churches
The United Holy Church of America

Biographical Index

Wilson, Aaron M. 217, 224
Wimber
    Carol 15, 16, 17
    John 13, 15-21
Wittich, Philip G. 147
Wood, George O. 11
Woodward, George 186
Woodworth-Etter, 173
  Maria
Wright, Joel Adams 209
Wuerch, Harry 125
Young, D.J. 55, 57
Youngren
    David 187, 188
    Peter 186-187, 188
Zaffuto
   Concettina (Pavia) 28
   Ferdinando 25, 27, 28, 30,
               31, 32
Zimmerman, Thomas F. 10

GENERAL INDEX